MONKEYS IN THE RAIN

Donna Carrère

SUMMERSDALE

Summersdale Publishers
46 West Street
Chichester
West Sussex
PO19 1RP
United Kingdom

www.summersdale.com

A CIP catalogue record for this book is available from the British Library.

Printed and bound in Great Britain.

ISBN 1 84024 154 3

For Rita Graves Brock, with love.

Contents

Preface 9

1. Heroic Indeed 15

2. One Heart Attack 22

3. Like We're in a Position 41

4. Foaming 50

5. Year of the Roasted Ear 65

6. Donna Loves Luana 82

7. Sleazebags Under My Eyes 93

8. How Many Dutchmen Does 109

it Take to Change a Sikh?

9. Why We Didn't Go to Singapore 118

10. Forsan Et Haec Olim Meminisse Iuvabit 134
(Perhaps some day even these things

will be pleasant to remember)

11. I Think My Mother Would

Like One of These Coathangers 149

12. Monkeys in the Rain 161

13. Hully Gully Blues Keep On Shuckin' 177

Epilogue 208

Perhaps it's the lunch that we had
Or the lunch that we should have had
But I am, in any case
A most inappropriate man
In a most unpropitious place

Wallace Stevens

Preface

A few words about dissatisfaction

My mother told me this anecdote from her hospital bed a few years ago: when I was six years old, her sister, a buyer for Neiman Marcus in Dallas, came over to say goodbye before taking off on a shopping trip to Paris and asked if there was anything special we wanted from France. To everyone's surprise, I pulled out an old babyfood jar from my toy box and demanded 'Dirt please . . . I'd like some French dirt.' My parents thought this was the most ignorant thing, but Auntie Ann remembered and found the time in her busy schedule to dig up a clod of earth from the Tuileries Gardens. When she gave it to me I unscrewed the lid, closed my eyes and inhaled ecstatically. From then on I kept this foreign country under my pillow, extracting it every night for a little snort before going to bed.

'Why in the world!' exclaimed my mother stiffly through her Parkinsonian mask. 'What ever were you thinking of?' I had no recollection of this extravagant behaviour but it sounded easy to explain.

'France, Mom – wouldn't you think?'

On this same nostalgic occasion – just before dying actually, and determined to prove one last time that I was the Bad Seed and sorely in need of a top-notch exorcist – she also revealed other childhood aberrations like sucking both thumbs at the same time, chronic orneriness and always being sick on Sundays.

'That's how come you're an atheist today,' she said, just the eyes blinking. 'It only goes to show . . .'

'I am not! Neither atheist nor agnostic. I've told you a million times I believe in the Cosmic Jokser.'

'Blasphemy!'

'Well I do. It's called freedom of religion Mom, guaranteed by the Constitution.'

'You are so disrespectful, it's more than that – you'll end up in hell if you don't watch out.'

It took a lot of frustrating growing up, but months before the reaching the legal age to drink (21) in Texas, I was already living, working and downing barrels of Beaujolais Nouveau in the eighteenth *arrondissement* of Paris. Happy little poor girl, an anarchist duckling chased out of her local puddle and suddenly floating, swimming, quacking and diving for *truite meunière* in the world's biggest reservoir of misfits: the city of Quasimodo, Marie Antoinette and Charles de Gaulle.

Strangely, it was the only place that had come to mind when I went through my identity crisis and had to find a refuge which would be far, fun and bad-girl friendly. If I was unaware of that dirt business, there was always a hunger for elsewhere *chez moi*, preferably abroad and with the offhand chance that I might possibly be able to communicate with the inhabitants – 'cause it sure wasn't happening in Dixie. I knew for a terrible fact that my family and maybe the whole community wanted me disappeared, skedaddled . . . gone with all my wind.

Chicken Chile Cheeseburgers and Slurpy Frosty Ooze Cones would never, ever be my food, Billy Graham my saviour, or, man! Ronald Fuck-a-Duck Reagan my president. I was persona-many-light-centuries-from-grata all the way up to second year in

college before it finally dawned: I was a closet alien!
My own personal splinter group!

So one decisive evening, following a bitter argument
about how many IQ points it didn't take an American
to wear a baseball cap, when mother said for the ten
thousandth time 'love it or leave it' . . . I left.

Now France was a country! The citizens enjoyed
excellent, practically free medical coverage. They were
sylph-like and elegant from eating well-balanced meals
of real food and not mass-produced, mushy, sugar and
cholesterol drenched slop. Racially mixed couples
abounded; indeed black, white, beige and yellow were
treated with equal disdain by the supercilious waiters
and sales clerks.

Communists headed the election lists in my
neighbourhood, Jesus was a much-beloved

Lyonnaise sausage, *les Pets de Nonne* – nun's farts
believe it or not – a traditional soufflé fritter, and Che
Guevara the name of half a dozen restaurants and cafés
in the metropolitan area. Best of all was the way they
all debated – whooee! – used their minds to figure
things out instead of waiting to be spoon-fed non-ideas
from the six o'clock news broadcasting clone. Bakers,
concièrges, bus drivers, grandmothers, dentists and
even light-hearted beauticians had learned – apparently
in the cradle – that eyes were not just for watching the
tube, but could be used to size up problems, discern,
compare and understand – their emotions were not
vestigial, nor their mouths uniquely loudspeakers for
prayer. *Les Français* were, to a person, politically savvy,
i.e. conscious of issues and sensitive to vacuous crap –
although in spite of their perspicacity (or because of

it), men and women could still sit down around a dinner table with casuistic adversaries to literally and figuratively chew the fat about the pros and cons of capital punishment or off an excellent *canard à l'orange*.

OK, now hold on tight and fast forward ten thousand English lessons into the future. So very many tête-a-têtes with corporate business people have done a lot to quell my natural Francophilia; not just because the majority of my adult students can't be bothered to apply themselves, coming as they do for the pleasant break it makes in their hectic work schedule, but due to the fact that in our ruthless, downsizing times, morality and decent human values seem to have been jettisoned in favour of survival and greed. Alas, this deflation in ethics poisons my classes and transforms our chats into one-sided monologues, since I can't very well tell a client that the earwax he keeps fiddling with during our conversation is just more of that shit he's got for brains.

To add insult to injury, these ardent chauvinists just do not consider the English language valid or serious enough to be embarrassed in, and consequently chatter on and on (badly), recounting various indiscretions and misdemeanours which they would never confess or admit willingly in their own tongue: the best way to punish a three week-old baby so she'll sleep through the night; how to avoid radar traps on the highway when drunk; why North African immigrants should be put in special camps; the boring details of their adulterous escapades; two or five or seven things they like about Le Pen, the xenophobic, right-wing extremist cyclops – *mais*, *attention*, nobody's racist here!

How had this happened so surreptitiously? Little by little and before my own loving eyes France had turned yucky! Charisma became charwasma . . .

Outside the classroom it was even worse, something like Mars in the house of Uranus. Terrorism was at its peak; rubbish bins and shopping bags were exploding all over the city and the air, smelling of lignite, vibrated with the wails of police and ambulance sirens. Sometimes these ambulances were carrying members of our own family, not ripped open by Carlos the Jackal, but dying of illness or battered and lacerated in accidents.

'Oooh, to be back in Bali or Jakarta,' sighed my husband eyeing our daughter's black rubber spiders. 'You've never lived till you've had roasted waterbugs on a stick.'

My fantasy was more prosaic, a reasonably peaceful and foreign land with a difficult language which would act as a buffer between me and the rest of humankind. Sweden sounded exotic and there was always North Africa, Turkey was especially tempting. But Pierre was always faithful to his own version of paradise:

'Probolinggo, Indramayu, Singaraja. You know what it's like to be served magic mushrooms with fried coriander chicken, go swimming later and see a shark coming straight at you?'

Then the internal revenue service wrongfully pursued us for a squillion francs; a greedy tourist sued Pierre and the museum director who employed him for taking unauthorised photos of him and his wife at an exhibit; Pierre got gout . . . it was endless hell on earth.

But one day it finally happened: we snapped as crisply as two breadsticks in the desert.

It was the evening our Greek friend, Yorgos, returned from holiday on a particularly remote island just south of the Pelopponese. Something about the way he recalled the charm and beauty of the place made us prick up our ears: shorter than average people – tiny really – dressed in black and grey, sitting splay-legged in orchards and munching raw asparagus. The housing market: 'For twenty dollar you buy a house – fifty you get a whole village.' (A bit of poetic license as it turned out.) And, 'Nobody tell the truth. Nothing. You say, "Is my wife outside?" they say, "No, she inside" but they know she go to the beach with the car. They like that.' Then he said the fatal words, 'Sperm trees.' Intriguing. 'Smell like a mushroom, you know?' explained George, 'You walk by that thing, you go "Aggggh", you like to fall down.'

That's all it took. We DID honestly swoon at the idea; milky musk was right there in the room with us – the promise of renewal. Or so we thought.

One more thing; some party poopers have felt the need to complain about our lack of direction, going so far as to label us 'flibbertigibbets' and dangerously capricious parents. This is false. We too have our beliefs and goals: The Cosmic Joker is our shepherd. The grass is always greener on the other side and . . . keep on sniffin'!

Chapter One

Heroic, Indeed

As we walked from the shuttle bus to the Bangkok airport terminal I could hear Pierre, two paces ahead of me, exclaim to our daughter, 'Ah, the wonderful, horrible heat! Look at my shirt . . . I'm the Sponge Man!'

It was January 19 and we had been flying all night, away from Greece and our newly adopted island which had, like the rest of the Common Market, just dropped its temperature down around its ankles. We were fleeing from the frozen water pump, the dim gas lights at five o'clock in the afternoon, and the hateful snow-rain that seeped into every crack in the house, turning our bread into pudding and us into irresponsible cowards.

'Let's get out of here,' I suggested one night as Pierre was jamming the bedroom window with one of my old nightgowns. 'This isn't Arcadia. This isn't the Greece that Gerald Durrell described. This is the Bronx!'

'But where can we go?' he asked, 'It's not warmer in France and besides, we don't have a house there any more.'

'I wasn't thinking of France,' I answered. 'We couldn't stay there during elections with all those bombs going off.'

'All right, but where *can* we go?' He had finished the windows and was now inserting batteries into our clip-on reading lamps.

'How about South East Asia?' I offered.

'You mean the one on the other side of the world?'

'Right.'

'OK.' He fastened his lamp onto his fisherman's cap, gave me mine, and climbed into bed.

'I just hope you understand,' he added, 'that it will mean spending all the money we have left in the bank, taking Ava out of school, giving her Greek, English, French, and mathematics lessons in trains, planes, buses, tricycles and risking hepatitis, polio, dysentery, cholera – and *all* of our credibility.'

'I know,' I answered, 'it's disconcerting.'

In the light of the next day, this idea, unlike others of its pedigree, was not the usual wraith that fluttered and collapsed after strong coffee and scrambled eggs; on the contrary, this one was the Godzilla that had us terrified, precisely because we knew that we'd go through with it.

Greece had left us exhausted and outraged by its local bureaucratic surrealism, cabalistic friendship rites, psychopathic workers, but most of all, by the extraterrestrial confusion concerning any information necessary to human life as we knew it.

Seven months previously we had decided to sue our destinies for ten years of back rent. A decade of toil, family illness, family wars, and general bad luck would be avenged by an old farm house on a little-known island in the Ionian, and the simpler, wiser life of say, the donkey, chewing and blinking in the sun.

We had fallen in love in Paris where I was an English teacher and Pierre was a photographer. Almost immediately we were forced to interrupt this idyll to look after three seriously ill parents. Somehow in the midst of strokes, Alzheimer's and cancer, Ava was born – although I can hardly remember when I even had time to go to the hospital.

A couple of years later a drunken tractor driver turned when Pierre was attempting to overtake him. I went through the windscreen. After my face was patched up and two parents eventually died – leaving a small inheritance – we decided to take the money and run. We would pool skills and transfer our headquarters to the paradise of our choice.

We had been to Greece on different occasions to recuperate, never getting enough of that heroic feeling in the air. We were going to grab some of that: go for the legend instead of the sit-com. We would give Romance a chance to transform our bad tempers into the radiant smiles of those staunch peasants working hand in hand with nature in faraway places. I would become friendly again and stay up nights preparing swollen moussakas for stray visitors. My kitchen would be sparse, containing only a wood stove, a table and chairs and a hefty knife for cutting up goats and things. Maybe Pierre would toss away his Nikons and get out his nets; if a picture was worth a thousand words, one medium-sized fish was worth its weight in gold, and the islanders didn't stall for six months before paying up, unlike the magazines and agencies in Paris.

So what had happened?

Alas, the Greece that had been so enchanting in her summer dress turned into a surly bag lady at the beginning of winter, a couch potato that couldn't even get up to heat herself a TV dinner.

Nobody had told us that it rained in Greece; that it would pour, day and night, for the whole month of November; or that we would have five inches of water in every room – except our bedroom – where we would have ten. It was never hinted at, that we would have to make six trips to Piraeus over a period of two months and pay a small fortune, just to change the license plates on our 12-year-old broken down Citroën.

And how could we have guessed that the workers we engaged to help us restore the house would refuse to come on: their mothers' saints' name day; good fishing days; the days the Big Boat arrived; the days the Big Boat left; the days they had to go to court to sue each other and the many, many days spent in the local hospital with unimaginable inconveniences. These included bee-stung nostrils, embedded fish-hooks, bleeding tear ducts and wisdom teeth emerging from tongues. The situation wasn't helped by the fact that the mason and the plumber couldn't stand each other, and therefore, our plaster was thrown on in the deepest anger and the sink pipes were forced obstinately into joints that were millimetres too small.

As for Ava, she should have been adapting well. Because we didn't live in town the council provided a taxi to take her to and from the one-roomed school where she was a pupil. Although nobody spoke either French or English, she was learning Greek at an incredible speed thanks to a devoted teacher and 11 talkative classmates. But from the beginning she was plagued (not unlike our workmen) by frustrating ailments: virulent conjunctivitis that puffed her eyelids into muffins; chunky little warts that had to be painfully burnt off; occasional strange fevers, darkly inflamed infections in scratches.

As we treated and consoled her month after month, it seemed as if this island was not only the first place that Aphrodite had visited after surfacing from the waves, according to Greek lore, but also the spot where Pandora had opened her notorious box of pestilence.

Things would have been easier if we'd had an alliance of friends, the solidarity of island dwellers floating along together; but from the end of August, just after the summer people and the tourists had all gone home, everybody we knew started going steadily berserk. Our next door neighbour let loose her 13 piglets who immediately took advantage of this pardon by charging into our courtyard, gobbling all the parsley and mint, destroying two water evacuation pipes and fouling up our front steps before charging off again into the olive groves. When I objected, our neighbour screamed that I should have a fence and gate like everybody else, and that it was perfectly normal for pre-pubescent pigs to cruise. It was 'Greek' – meaning that I was *not*.

Two weeks later, my beer-drinking, best-island-friend stopped speaking to me because – according to her husband – every time I came to visit something *died*! Whatever I admired either broke or withered or was found mauled to death the next morning! Me? With my collection of *Mad Magazine* and my recipes for clam chowder and pecan twists?

After this, a German friend fell triumphantly in love with Pierre. We just weren't expecting it. We had known her for six summers and she had hardly ever glanced at *him*, but would swoop down on *me* at all hours of the day to discuss medical misinformation, which happened to be both our specialities. So, wasn't Pierre astonished when she started sitting next to him at parties, grabbing his thigh when he said something funny and asking him to help pull her generator in the evening. Generator-pulling was inevitably interrupted for a couple of hours of sundown whiskies and cosy 'meaning of life' chats.

All of this eventually reached a point of no return when he found an unstamped letter in the local post office reading 'Meet me behind the olive oil factory at midnight'.

After all the hours we'd spent discussing uterus malfunctions, and all the articles I'd saved her about kidney transplants and dialysis machines. Of course Pierre was nowhere near the olive oil factory at midnight and the next thing we knew she was spreading rumours that he fished with dynamite.

Then, around Christmas, the basic structure of the island collapsed: the sea turned menacing and we received no more vegetables, coffee or milk. Maybe it was withdrawal, but every single person on the island became ill and since the only pharmacist had left for a short trip to Athens and couldn't get back, we could be diagnosed in the tiny hospital, we could even get sympathy from the doctors, but we couldn't be cured because we couldn't get into the pharmacy.

A couple of weeks later, the boat carrying our precious butane gas bottles foundered off the west coast of the Peloponnese, so we couldn't cook anything except some very musky stews over the coal fire. We tried going to the restaurant but this place mysteriously stopped serving its usual fare of pizzas and grilled indigenous chops, and concentrated instead on breaded, deep-fried liver and chips which nobody with a twentieth century stomach could possibly digest. The population went into a deep funk when this restaurant – which was also the local bar – decided to offer cold, left over, deep-fried liver cubes for the cocktail snacks that accompanied the ouzo and the beer in the evening.

At the beginning of January there was absolutely no reason to rise in the morning, except to kindle a small, arbitrary irritation – anything would do, a broken tap, the weather, the persistent tinkle of sheep bells – and keep it glowing until nightfall.

Pierre and I were ready to leave, fed up, seething, out to alienate, blaspheme, cut loose. We were ready to boogie.

Chapter Two

One Heart Attack

Customs, which we had been warned about, was as easy as a cha-cha-cha: we advanced, they stepped back, we shifted, they lurched forward, and then we all came together. Were we not *personae ultra gratae* with our new haircuts, our sun-dressed child, and the balance of our savings account stuffed into wallets that bulged like moneyburgers? The joyous visa officer stamped our passports with a two week transit visa, which was more than enough since we would be leaving Thailand in a few days to explore Malaysia. After handing us back the documents he came out to our side of the counter, patted Ava on the shoulder and said, 'You are a little girl.'

Descending on the escalator in the cool hall of the airport, we floated into a tumult of taxi drivers, all beseeching us to *come*:

'Come, now.'

'Come you, here, please.'

'Come, baby, Bangkok to.'

'Come my taxi, much little money!'

This was a considerable change from Athens where you had to run screaming after yellow cabs, begging them to at least slow down and consider. We chose one enthusiastic-looking driver, mainly because of his T-shirt which rejoiced in four inch letters: 'THAILAND IS GOOD FOR YOU'. He bowed to us, took some of the luggage and winked at Ava, but, when he finally opened his mouth to speak, the verbal turmoil made my head spin.

'You like go down up good hotel big street Coke drink nice for baby?'

'Hotel, little money, big room, big cold, very beautiful,' I requested.

'Thank you, sir,' he salaamed and smiling, ushered us into a roomy Toyota that was about the temperature of Leningrad. We were comfortable, groggily happy, and for half an hour scanned the billboards along the highway for clues to the city we were approaching. If they were any indication, Bangkok was a place governed by yin-yang concepts: Coca-Cola and Pepsi Cola. Their profusion was equal, their importance blatant, and for miles of highway they fought out the concept of 'light' in colour combinations I'd never seen before.

As we entered the city a rush of traffic gobbled us up and our driver swivelled his head 90 degrees to yell excitedly, 'Bangkok, too much bus!'

After we had agreed and he had re-agreed, we stopped for a traffic light that lasted through half his tape deck of Michael Jackson's *Greatest Hits*. At first we thought there had been an accident, then Pierre said something about an electrical breakdown. However, when our chauffeur left to get a bowl of noodles at the curb, I guessed that we were only knee deep in a culture gap and this could just possibly be Asia.

Once we started moving again the flow accelerated and we sped past wooden houses with wide panels flung open to reveal whole families moping around, eating, sleeping, watching television, eating, serving customers, unloading merchandise, bowing at passers-by, beheading chickens and – eating.

We began to notice the fabulous number of three-wheeled motorbike taxis decorated in chrome and plastic whose rear-view mirrors jiggled with amulets and garlands of flowers. Some were bulging with up to half a dozen diminutive Thais and some were just full of one big tourist.

A quarter of an hour later, we pulled up to a kind of Spacelab: a gigantic futuristic hotel consisting of a thrusting, grandiose array of every building material possible, and heralded by an asymmetric archway which doubled as a rainbow-coloured waterfall.

'No good. No good!' cried Pierre, imagining multinational vice-presidents and Gucci bags. Off we rode again, honking past embassies and temples until we arrived at a delightful Tudor façade, half hidden by orchards and reflected in a friendly swimming pool. The lobby was draped and the furniture covered in flowery chintz. The flower-papered walls boasted bird-dog illustrations and official pictures of the British Royal Family. It wasn't 100 per cent Oriental, but the rates were good and besides, we were becoming severely travel warped.

Five minutes after taking possession of the room and losing our shoes in the pampas-like carpet, Pierre began to tremble and gasp; he turned ashen, and in a few seconds his clothes were plastered with sweat against his body. Ava and I watched this metamorphosis with our mouths hanging open – I could only marvel at the velocity of the local amoebae. We had been on Thai soil for a little more than two hours; it was as if a

Saronged Reaper had met us at the airport – and beckoned.

'Lie down!' I ordered. 'Something endemic is invading you.'

He sprawled out on the bed and smiled. 'This is nothing but travel malaise. It's the change of climate, the thirteen-hour fear of crashing, but most of all, the alcohol from the plane, the scotches and wines and beers. This is just an unusual hangover, you'll see. You had as much, if not more.'

'Pierre, are you trying to tell me that *you* have *travel tremens*! We only had three little scotches each – over a night and a day. That doesn't turn you into a dripping tapioca!'

'Tapioca doesn't drip. What's in the fridge?'

Ava opened the miniature door and rattled off a litany of familiar and not so familiar beverages: Sprite, Coca-Cola, B-152, Fanta, Polaris, White-Spring Water, Mekong Whisky.

'Mekong Whisky! Youpie! I'm back!' he yelled, but I wasn't convinced.

'I'm going to call the desk and ask for a doctor.'

'Give me fifteen minutes,' he said confidently, 'and I'll be fine. I want to go out.'

Equally washed out, I lay on the opposite bed and stared at a picture of a heavily-bonneted Princess Anne christening a ship.

'Let's play tic-tac-toe,' Ava suggested, with the infinite recuperative powers of the eight-year-old nervous system. And sure enough, after 20 minutes of bleary-eyed X-ing and O-ing, I was startled back into reality by grunts from Pierre's bed. He stretched and harrumphed, smacked his lips, leaped up in front of the mirror and proceeded to run his hands through his hair, undress, shower and revive. The fever was gone, his fingers were firm on his buttons: he was a whole Frenchman again.

We decided to take a scooter to Chinatown and climbed into one of the 12 *samlors* that immediately appeared as we stepped out of the hotel. The driver was raucous with laughter at the sight of us and kept adjusting his rear view mirror, then exploding into silent giggles. I hoped this was an isolated phenomenon because if we provoked this as a general reaction, sightseeing was going to be very uncomfortable.

In between chortles he stroked and pulled in the region of his crotch, gasping and shimmying with erratic up and down thrusts of his hand. Swift Cartesian reckoning pushed me to the barbed-wired frontiers of sanity: could it be common here to fondle oneself in public and to embarrass already disorientated tourists? Could this be part of the perverted aura of Bangkok, world capital of creative sin? I nudged Pierre and pointed to the busy thigh area, but he just shrugged and I thought, *Well, he's been here before*. It wasn't until we stopped for a red light and the driver leaned back that I realised he had only been manoeuvring the gear stick which stuck its little rounded plastic head right up next to his groin, joining him in a pleasant symbiotic relationship to the motor – my only excuse being that I was stupidly tired.

The traffic was intense and monstrous. The sun had set, liberating what seemed like ninety million workers from their towers and fifty million tourists from the debilitating heat. Buses and taxis sighed out great nimbuses of black exhaust fumes and the cracked-voice burps from the scooters went straight to our brain roots and then out again, echoing against the giant skyscrapers and mega-galactic hotels.

As we eased our way into the swarming streets and alleys of Chinese vendors, Ava suddenly perked up and shouted: 'Invisible noodles! Invisible noodles!'

She wasn't delirious but only confusing the words 'transparent' and 'invisible', for, about two and a half metres away, stood an enormous glass vat of glowing, warm, green spaghettini, twinkling and crackling like special effects from the *Amityville Horror*. It was a perfect place to stop, so we paid the driver who permitted himself a parting 'Hello!' and pushed ourselves into a torrent of frenzied shoppers.

Every inch of the pavement and curb, the doors and the serpentine passages, was occupied by one enterprise or another: meatballs, false teeth, hair pins, dried fish, Donald Duck Walkmans, red hard-boiled eggs, woks, silver soups, ravioli, and bikinis with Madonna heads on the bra cups. We passed pharmacies stocked with dried rodents, mountainous assortments of pickled claws and tongues, rows of interspecied organs, puckered testicles, bottles of multicoloured slime, candy jars of teeth, fangs, tails and appendages. We had to leap over beggars and infants that had, somehow, managed to squeeze themselves into the throngs and lay in spaced-out oblivion, their backs against juice stalls and knees twisted to the flow of the crowd. There were also disfigured men and children with deep holes in their faces.

We wandered down a side street, off the main road, in search of a food stall, but all we found were dark, smoky stands of sizzling innards and suspended roasted ears.

When I asked Pierre what he thought, Ava began to sniffle and protest.

'I don't want to eat ears. I'm not used to it.'

'Don't worry,' I reassured her, 'nobody's in the mood for ears. We'll turn back and go to one of those restaurants on the avenue.'

As we approached the lighted area, a dirty dog sidled up to us. His legs and muzzle were painted blue and he had amulets around his neck and bells on his feet. He gave us a long, deliberate stare and then – I know this sounds ridiculous – he stood on his hind legs, stretched out his left paw to Ava's shoulder and closed his eyes. Had we met before?

Were we hallucinating? Were there such profound and disturbing strains of jet-lag that they bordered on the paranormal? Pierre was doubtful.

'He's simply a very discriminating Buddhist dog.'

Ava was in thrall over this dream she was having. *'Je t'aime,'* she whispered to him, and I had to dissuade her from hugging him around the neck.

We chose a spacious gymnasium of a café, but the minute we entered all pandemonium erupted. It was like the Beatles arriving in New York; everyone started scurrying around us, shouting in monosyllables and pointing to the steaming displays of pots and cauldrons. A waiter took Pierre's arm and led him towards the pans while another pushed me to a front window table. They had overlooked Ava who stood at the entrance, not knowing whether to laugh or cry. From the look on her face I figured she was tic-tac-toeing in her head. It occurred to me that she might have a natural talent for travel.

After a few minutes of swatting and protesting and demanding and refusing we tucked into roast duck on a bed of black mushrooms, garnished with unidentifiable yellow triangles which Ava and Pierre skipped, but which I found to have a delightful *je ne sais quoi* of Ray Bradbury. As a gesture of good will, the waiter offered us a free plate of something black and hairy and we had to pat our stomachs to mime that we had had more than enough, until, shaking his head, he took it back to the kitchen.

The best part of the meal though, was the seraphic Singha beer, light and coquettish, like a thousand jokes erupting in the bloodstream. It left a good 20-minute after-glow, during which time we wandered the avenue, browsing through stalls, barely seeing, barely breathing; just alive and there.

By this time we were so tired we were almost tempted to crawl into a corner with the beggars. In the tuk-tuk back to the hotel, we passed many a strange sight. It seemed as if Bangkok was the stage for an all-encompassing avant-garde play and we were surrounded by the actors: three little women pushing an empty municipal bus down a busy avenue; a metallic grey coffin lying on top of a metallic grey Nissan and a tipsy American woman (who looked like Mamie Eisenhower) alone in another tuk-tuk, singing 'Hit the road, Jack'.

I don't know how we managed to get back to our beds – maybe a few Thai porters carried us up and tuk-tuked us in – but I can remember waking up at three in the morning and groping my way to the bathroom for a sleeping pill; I had no intention of tossing and turning through the thousand impressions of the last two days. As I inched my way back through the unfamiliar sheets, I felt something wet and spongy, like an angel-food cake that has been left in the fridge too long. It was Pierre.

The following morning when I opened my eyes, I could see Ava in the bathroom playing with the complimentary shower cap, and her father standing and staring at the thermometer in his hand.

'Look at this,' he marvelled, '39.7!'

'Right,' I decided, jumping out of bed. 'I'm calling the airport and we're going home! We don't stand a chance in this country, we haven't been here twenty-four hours and you're . . . you're exuding . . . you're dripping wet!'

'We can at least have breakfast,' he said and reached for the phone. He got the receptionist and read off directly from the room menu:

'Two pots dripping coffee, one glass of boil milk, three crisp toasts under country butter.'

However, when he hung up, he really started to shake and didn't seem to have enough hands to press the pains in his arms and his chest and his head.

'It's nothing,' he mumbled.

We silently got dressed, grabbed our passports and money, and went downstairs to ask directions to the nearest hospital.

In the taxi he tried to think of some explanation for this sudden turn of events.

'It's probably from carrying all that luggage. The strap of that bag with all the books in it left a red mark on my shoulder. Listen, we're both in a fragile post-aerian condition. I'm sure there's nothing wrong with me – I'm going to look pretty silly when they diagnose acute travel hysteria and aggravated muscle reverse.'

He was starting to babble.

The Saint Louis Hospital's first great advantage was that it existed. Its second quality was a resemblance to the Pentagon's Ballistics Department: no-nonsense, computer run, death – frowned upon. They whisked us in, took Pierre's name and passport number and in five minutes swooped him away to be examined, X-rayed, tested, probed and delved. Ava and I sat in the hall watching Thais be sick and studying the nurses' wide variety of sexy uniforms. The rule was 'green' but in any shape or style: green shantung sheaths, light green saris, green sarongs with pea green sheer blouses, green sleeveless cotton sweaters with green split skirts. They made me think of one of Ava's first children's books like *The Vegetable's Birthday Party* or *Mary Rose in the Land of the Green Fairies*.

We went for a walk around the circular terraces of the garden adjoining the sick rooms. Magnolias, cyclamen and palm trees lined the arcades that peeped onto small aviaries. There was a spaciousness unheard of in the cramped quarters of European hospitals, not to mention the deplorable slum projects they send you to in New York.

When we returned to the hall, Pierre appeared with lots of papers, and a beautiful girl wearing a rather transparent green silk shirt-dress. She smiled at me as if to announce that I had just won the biggest lottery of the century. Her flawless dusky cheeks dimpled and her eyes shone with every promise on Buddha's palette.

'Sir,' she said breathlessly, 'you husband, he just have one heart attack. It is not so important, but very serious. Doctor say we keep him to see he doesn't to die.'

'*My God*!' I screamed and then I couldn't see anything because I was crying so hard. Then Ava started crying and Pierre started crying and the nurses started laughing, clapping their hands and rocking back and forth on their heels.

This green bouquet of women gathered around us, intrigued by so much drama. They giggled and jostled each other and pulled Ava's ponytail which made her sob even louder. Eventually we all moved off down the corridor to escort Pierre to the Cardiac Wing.

What was a heart attack? I wondered. I didn't know heart attacks. I had thought that only travelling salesmen or small-aircraft pilots or dishonest senators had heart attacks. Pierre was a babyish 42; his heart was still in love! What could this be?

Ava and I stood outside his room while the nurse helped him out of his stone-washed, drip-dry travel jeans, and forced him into Thai wraparound work trousers and a kimono top. He looked pained, frightened and in my strained and bewildered mind I kept hearing the words of a popular song, 'a total eclipse of the heart.'

When he was officially installed, I went and sat by the bed.

'What exactly did the doctor say?' I wanted to know. I had a terrible headache, Pierre kept changing colours and Ava was slumped on a grey wicker chair, looking like a battered Cabbage Patch doll.

'It's definitely a heart attack by the electrocardiogram,' he said, 'but we have to make more tests to see how much damage there's been and if there'll be any scar tissue.'

'But is it over? Will there be any more? I mean are they like earthquakes?'

'I don't know.'

'But why did it happen?'

'I don't know.'

'Will the doctor be able to say?'

'Probably. I just don't know.'

We stared at each other, trying to remember who we were. The door opened and an authoritative but cavalier sister, wearing a starched white wimple, strutted in. She grinned, looked us over and quickly decided that I was dispensable.

'You go away – now. You husband must rest before we give him lots of tests. You come back night. How you like Thailand?'

Pierre, risking another coronary incident, guffawed.

'It's an exciting country,' I replied.

I kissed him and inanely pulled up his sheet – it was about 90 degrees under the overhead fan. Ava stood up to ask him which side the heart was on, and when he told her she bent over and kissed the breast pocket of his shirt. I had already seen this in *The Champ*, starring Wallace Beery and Jackie Cooper: we were in serious melodrama here.

'OK. See you later – let's go Ava. We'll have to get him some newspapers and paper dolls and things.'

I tried to be blithe but my voice sounded accented, Norwegian, as if the consonants were torturing the vowels.

Outside it was 512 degrees in the midday sun. We climbed into an empty tuk-tuk, but when the driver turned to ask us for our destination, I couldn't tell him where to go – it hadn't occurred to me to take down the address of the hotel. I knew the name, but as it was not one of the landmarks like the Rama Dama or the Almighty Imperial Palace, the driver was as lost as I was in the immensity that was Bangkok.

Instead of crying again, which I wanted to do very badly, I remembered what my mother used to tell me when I was a little girl:

'Whenever you find yourself in a particularly difficult situation, spell Mississippi twice, forward and backward.' After completing this exercise, I took a deep breath and tried to think.

'How much to TAT?' I asked after a few seconds. It was the only name I had retained from the *Hitchhiker's Guide to Thailand* – the Thai Association of Tourism. It just went to show that, as an American, I would be forever dependent on jingles, slogans and cute little abbreviations that fit into my bite-sized brain slots like indestructible pinballs.

He demanded an outrageous 90 baht but I was too miserable to take on the robust activity of bargaining. 'Whatever,' I sighed, and we *varoomed* off on little wheels into the horrendous bowels of noon traffic.

There was no doubt about it, this was a car's world; passenger vehicles, taxis and minibuses, all had smoked, darkened windows, so the effect was of driverless, empty automobiles in mechanical ritual, claiming the streets, dominating the city. The tuk-tuks just emphasised this diminished humanity as their drivers manoeuvred, sweated and struggled with hiccuping motors while passengers hung over the back seats hyperventilating.

When we arrived at the TAT building our bodies were poached and curdled and we had a few unpleasant moments ungluing ourselves from the plastic covers; Ava's eyes were rolling around in their sockets and I was crying again. Once inside it was cool and some superior, all-knowing angel of mercy led us to a desk, where a Mother Theresa of abused tourists calmed me down with tea and force-fed me with information. She wrote out the name and address of our hotel in Thai script for all future drivers. Then she gave me brochures for outings: the Crocodile Farm, the Snake Farm, the Wats, boat rides on the klongs, the Chinese opera. I leaned back, letting therapeutic air-conditioning massage my nerve endings.

I must have looked abnormally helpless because she inclined her head and asked, 'Would you prefer a personal guide? They are very experts. They can show you the meaning of Bangkok.'

It was an enchanting proposition but I was not sure I needed that knowledge. I thanked her and went to retrieve Ava, who had been kidnapped by a flock of maternal secretaries and was being stuffed with ginger-flavoured hard candies.

Back into the jungle and an uneventful cab-ride to the hotel, which at this point looked like 'Grandma's house over the hill', our only known factor in Bangkok, the place where our books and knickers marked our territory.

We went directly to the dining-room where we sank into window seats that were more like lovers than chairs: the cushions – thick with modern chemical softness – crawled up our backs, trying to make amends for the miseries of the day. The heavy silver and the thick linen tablecloth suggested security, giving off the message that there was still some ballast left in the world.

As we ordered and waited for our lunch, a never-ending medley of American Bandstand favourites I hadn't heard in 30 years, came slinking over the loudspeakers, successfully cloned by feathery Thai voices: 'Dream', 'Travelling Man', 'Mr Blue', 'Diana', 'Will You Love Me Tomorrow?' These whispers from the past sounded like mysterious symbols that were threading together to give me a sign of what was happening. What *was* happening?

The waiter brought us the food and Ava tried to explain why she didn't like Chinese soups.

'When they're clear and have things that float sideways, it makes me dizzy and my teeth hurt.'

I considered this; maybe it had something to do with the monosodium glutamate content.

'But, Ava,' I said, 'the things that float are the things you like – mushrooms, chicken bits, tomatoes. What difference does it make if they float or just sit in the bottom?'

'It's just not nice.'

For three hours we flopped around the hotel room like beached whales, the way restless women do, waiting for the bastard sun to drop dead. There's no other way to describe that intimidating glow. Only when the Venetian blinds attained a certain ecru shading did we strike out for the hospital.

This time, after reading the Thai writing, which spelled out very clearly 'Saint Louis Hospital', the driver proceeded to take us about 10 kilometres out of our way, and pulled up in front of a rambling colonial house with a door sign that read : THE MARIA ROTHMAN SHINER MATERNITY HOME. I had to point and draw and question several people on the street before we could take off again.

Pierre was sleeping when we arrived at the hospital, but the doctor was present and asked me to follow him into his office. He was a congenial 40-year-old with rimless glasses and a general air of 'whizz kid' about him. When he sat down he smiled so sweetly that I thought, *This can't be a doctor*, but the multiple diplomas on the wall behind him reassured me.

'Your husband,' he said in quaint, embroidered English, 'is suffering by way of arteriosclerosis, a narrowing of his arteries. He must be very considerate from now on – no smoking, no fat animals, special diet and a lot of hard bed rest. Please, madam, there must be no physical commerce for as long as six weeks. When he is a little better, you will return home for further consultation and care.'

Home. Home was a Greek island where the local hospitalette had already rushed Ava by plane to Athens for an emergency appendectomy, only to discover, on arrival, that she had severe tonsillitis. Home was where the island doctors sat behind big mahogany desks eating pitta sandwiches, while you pulled down your pants to show your left buttock, which was canary yellow and swollen to three times the size of your right buttock.

All of this was complicated, but the cardiologist listened to me with superhuman patience as I explained our need to stay put for as long as it took Pierre to recover, and/or for spring to hit Greece. It would mean getting a visa extension first of all, something the Thai officials hated to do most in this world (according to the guidebook). We had only 12 days left on our passports and we obviously needed more than that. Dr Somiak Hoonponosimament dutifully reached for his pen and wrote a lengthy and terrible medical certificate, guaranteed to armbend any bureaucrat into submission.

But I had other questions: What about alcohol? And spices? Could he have a follow-up second attack? Would he be better or was it chronic? What about laughing? What about pulling the cord on the water pump? The doctor looked at me with some concern, but his words were smiling.

'A little alcohol is good for his problem – not too much. Spices must be limited – there might be intestinal complications; it's nice for him to laugh but there must not be no personal physical effort for at least a month. No package over five kilograms.'

At this point two nurses entered the room and stood effacing themselves in the corner. They tittered and shushed and chuckled and whispered while the doctor went on about blood clots and cholesterol. The combination of his diplomatic warnings and the nurses' houri-like natter was jarring and under the strain of the last 48 or 39 or 72 hours, or however long it had been, I whirled around and glared at them. Their reaction, however, was of the Orient: they blinked in surprise, then stepped forward to bow with their hands together. One of them patted my head while the other said pleasantly, 'Your brother is woke up sir, she wants to see you.'

Having delivered this message, they stationed themselves on either side of the doctor, and all three of them laughed me out the door.

Pierre was weakly grumpy. The first thing they had done was wash him vigorously, although he protested that he had already had two showers since he arrived.

'Three of them came in,' he complained, 'with pans and brushes and towels, like I was a race horse or something, and, believe me, they left no stone unturned. Besides that, they gave me a kind of belly and heart soup garnished with floating stars. Then, a French chaplain came in and asked if I needed *un ami*! *Merde!*'

'Please don't get worked up,' I soothed. 'You're getting a rare inside view of an exotic country.'

Ava was in bed with him by this time, with the covers pulled up and reading her paperback. The door opened and a whole new cortège of green beauties crowded into the room. When they saw Ava and Pierre reading together they couldn't stand it; they gasped and surrounded the bed, caressing and squeezing cheeks. One gracious handmaiden bent over Pierre and looked into his eyes.

'I like it when you smiles,' she said.

He squinted at me sideways like a satisfied reptile. I thought maybe things would get better.

Chapter Three

Like We're in a Position

Every day Ava and I plodded across Bangkok, either by scooter, taxi or – God help us – on foot. We were always against the current, always exerting. We were married to the traffic, dwarfed by the jumble of high-tech rises, persecuted by the monotonous, omnipresent drone, like a ship's generator, that fills the city's steamy air. In Bangkok there is no sense of neighbourhood, only 'carhood', and it appeared that the city was waiting resignedly for complete automotive checkmate in the very near future.

According to the *Bangkok Post*, 90 per cent of all cars registered in Thailand never left Bangkok and the rate of car sales was much higher than the rate of road construction. These two statistics, combined with the fact that all cars were permanently in motion, made it almost certain that sooner or later they would stop for a light, en masse, and nobody would ever move again.

We struggled along the boulevards and avenues, humbled and dishonoured by the heat and the city's vast natural wealth of carbon monoxide, but, more than everything else, by the noise: the exclamations of triumphant motors at home among themselves.

Usually, when you go out in a new city – or any city for that matter – you have a sense of speculation, a feeling of the prowl, the hunt; your body is living in the open and you feel physical or raffish or intrepid. An adventure is guaranteed. A city is where anomalies pile up and unless you're suffering from advanced apathy or a raging hangover something will always happen, some little wonder whose memory sticks to you like milk stains over the upper lip. But in Bangkok, once you cross the threshold of your air-conditioned shelter, there is a *whoosh* like the sucked-in gasp of an atomic explosion, and then a droning, alarming fallout of noise particles that turns you into an instant mutant. It's as if 45 new ears sprouted on your head all at once, sharp and receptive to every level of sonic vibration, from the mean purring of heavy diesel engines to the tinkling clatter of the thirty-five billion pots and pans of the Bangkok food force, to unnameable bangs and gongs of Asian living.

Once you start walking, the acoustics spiral around your head like a moonshine still, fermenting the brain until little bubbles of carbonation percolate under your skull, and your mouth becomes an oblong 'O' like in the Munch painting of 'The Scream'. The only adventure you can have is simply a stroke. Your overall purpose is to get to your destination at once, with the urgency of the ambulance driver zooming towards the emergency ward. There is no possibility of strolling or browsing or even stopping to ask the time; your gait is the lunge, the hurtle, the propeller movement.

There is also another distressing element: the Techno Factor. Having matured musically in the glorious seventies, there is nothing, to me, that spells 'chicken shit' more neatly than classic techno, with its dumb, tedious beat of copulating dogs and those lame-brained stutterings, 'Oh, oh I think I got it, got it, I think I got it, I think, I think I got it, got it, got it.'

This is the Bangkok beat, the perfect rhythm for synchronising the millions of workers in their tiny occupations: hawking shoe laces, ladling out soup, peeling fruit, cutting fifty trillion microscopic chunks of satay meat, sweeping, collecting cigarette butts, petal threading for garlands, toothpick whittling, and so on. Techno with the relentless cadence of a sewing machine, attaches these toilers to their daily lot like sequins on a go-go dress. The big Bangkok shimmy.

The first wat we visited was only a few steps from our hotel, in a grimy car repair district where people actually lived on the work sites. Hair brushes lay side by side with wrenches, white shirts were hung up to dry next to stacks of damaged tyres, and in one hangar a pink ruffled bassinet was suspended over a broken down motor. Everyone was black; two-year-olds crawled through sludge and their mothers wore starched white stained shirts and blouses. Sometimes the cavernous shops doubled as diners, proposing big sooty cauldrons of soups and ravioli, or roast chickens propped up next to exhaust pipes. And everywhere – in front of pumps on the streets and in the temples – were hard-boiled eggs piled on display, stacked in grosses, and most often painted red.

Turning right on this garage-lined street, we entered a walled off compound overflowing with stray dogs, baby monks and special sacrifice stands where hawkers sold flower necklaces, golden coins, ginger cakes, incense and even little plastic bags of Coca-Cola (fastened at the top with a rubber band and a straw sticking out). At first I was indignant: why not sacrifice a pile of compact discs or a brand new pair of Adidas? Sacrifices were supposed to be ethereal, beauteous, but here you had Coca-Cola, always on time, just making another buck.

The more I thought about it however, the more I began to realise that in Thailand, Coke *was* sacred: a sub-religion. Actually it was more like a divine battle between Coke and Pepsi, with Coke in the role of the jihad Moslems while the more enlightened Pepsi bided its time in the background. People wore Coca-Cola T-shirts, baseball caps and shoulder bags; drivers dangled foam-rubber bottles from their rear-view mirrors; there were tiny Coca-Cola earrings for pierced ears. One day, visiting the silent grounds that isolate the extraordinary temple of Wat Po, we turned to go up the stairs and were jolted from our trance of infinite beauty by a very large sign which blurted: 'NO SPITTING – IT'S DISGUSTING. COMPLIMENTS OF COCA-COLA.' Another sign at the exit read: 'PLEASE PUT YOUR REFUSE IN THIS RECEPTACLE DONATED BY PEPSI'.

There were national volleyball teams that compete on TV – red uniforms for Coke and black ones for Pepsi with the fans dressed correspondingly. I thought it might have something to do with carbonation, that slight kick you get after guzzling a glassful. Perhaps it was akin to Buddhist euphoria, a short cut to hilarity. I thought about the soft drink addicts here: the Thais were spacey, always merry, as if they'd had a massive secretion of peptids, those enzymes that protect us from pain. And what if those enzymes met up with carbonation and . . .

Anyway, after passing the oblations we turned a corner and came up short before our first prodigious

Buddha: elongated, 60 feet high and covered in gold leaf. This was like caviar to the eyes, a visual succour; it was discovering, finally, what was important in life: gold! Ava was very willing to take off her shoes in order to approach the altar and to present him with a plate of cakes.

It was balmy here, a refuge from the battlefields outside the walls. We sauntered past the guest book and took a look at the tourists remarks:

This is a wonderful work of art. Keep up the good work.
Mrs Edward Louis, Dickson, Virginia.

Glorious are the marvels of this strange land.
Dr. Maurice Linkletter – Toronto, Ca . . .

Across the gravelled alley was a smaller, less ornate temple that sat modestly in the shadows of the colossal Buddha. Once again we took off our shoes and padded into the main altar room.

I was examining the painted figures on the wooden panels of the door when Ava, who was always a few leagues in advance, came running back to whisper in a low roar, 'Maman. *Regarde!*'

My eyes followed her index finger and fell upon a stuffed, embalmed or sun-dried bonze: an ancient monk sitting in a very fixed lotus position inside a glass case. He was long, long dead and artfully preserved but didn't look particularly transcended, only resigned to being on display. Some true believers came in, walking on their knees across the marble floor, chanting and bowing until they reached the holy mummy, at which point they prostrated themselves and accelerating the tone, entreated, begged, cajoled and remonstrated simultaneously. I would have had second thoughts about asking him for anything; I didn't really appreciate his deadness or his uncanny physical resemblance to George Bush.

It is wonderful how fast the nervous system can accommodate itself to the strangest new circumstances, how quickly a person can set up new routes, guideposts, habits.

By the third day of Pierre's hospitalisation, I was criss-crossing the city like a politician on the campaign trail. Wherever Ava and I went, we had intense, down to earth chats with all citizens; the urgency of our situation and the extremities of weather dictated bulldozer attitudes and proscribed the 'wait until we get used to the people' policy. Whereas in Greece I had avoided any contact with the unknown person, for fear of a snub or a contemptuous dismissal, here I was at ease, one of the gang. I felt like I had a couple of million *very* good friends.

For example, when I asked the saleslady at the Alliance Française Bookshop (where Ava loved to go and breathe in all things French) if I could leave my daughter there in the afternoon while I went to the hospital to visit her father, all generosity broke loose. The girl said, 'Oh, no problem sir', fetched a deckchair from the back-room, picked up a handful of boiled sweets on her way back and set Ava up like a miniature Gertrude Stein in her own little salon in the far end of the store. In the course of the afternoon and others to follow, she would bring Ava fresh orange juice from the canteen next door, share plates of chicken and rice with her, and eventually teach her Thai proverbs such as, 'When in a town where people wink, you must also wink' and 'Don't make bamboo water containers before you see the river'.

When I had set up a modicum of organisation and once again felt sense oozing around my life, I eased my blinkers off and began to notice things, things that persisted in forcing themselves to my attention, that itched in the corners of my eyes like painful shards, things that I can only describe as terminally sickening.

We were in the hotel restaurant, deeply involved in garlic shrimps and stuffed chicken wings, sitting back to back with some glistening American jocks, just out of the swimming pool, apparently refreshed and terribly, terribly lucid.

'Like she didn't even know how to kiss,' one of them honked over my shoulder. I shifted my chewing to second gear and listened.

'Her teeth like bumped against mine. She was so shy. I mean, man, they're so trusting and they meet these bastards, these creeps, these losers, they just think they're God's gift! It's no wonder foreign guys get a bad reputation. I mean like us, we're the good guys, let's face it. We go into a bar, we start talking, like we've got a sense of humour, we're fun, right? We're nice. We are human beings, right? OK, so we have a few drinks and dance, and then we're feeling good, right? And we want some company – which is normal – but we play fair, nothing kinky. Am I right?'

'Yeah,' agreed another. 'I've been going with this girl, Torong, you know, it's like a Thai name, it's common. I'm thinking about paying for her to get typing lessons. I want to help her, you know? Like we're in a position?'

'I know, I know what you're saying. You remember Suzy, the one I was with last week? She's a real good gal, stayed with her all weekend. You know how much I gave her? Thirty five dollars! Can you believe it? She's a good gal, though. And I forgot – listen to this – she cooked practically all the meals and she washed and ironed my clothes, like it was a pleasure for her. Maybe I'll buy her a Walkman or something. I don't know.'

My stuffed chicken wing was sticking in my glottis membrane. These boys were, at the most, 23 years old. Philosophers all. These were madras jackets talking, khaki bermudas spewing forth. I think that having their hair airbrushed and sculpted weekly was the determining factor, a liberalising influence. These were the cleanest males of any species, jump starting their consciences.

From then on, I started to pay attention, to gawp really, at the massive foreign consumption of Thai girls. No matter how old they actually were, none appeared more than 14. They were delicate, passive and 100 per cent government issue, distributed at the airport like leis in Hawaii, the national product of Thailand. The Thais have a name for them, 'Those Who Must Eat', because most of them come from the north east were the land is poor and the people starving. They are sold by their families, or rented, or leased to Bangkok distributors who line them up like T-bones in Dallas, like pork chops in Munich, and prime them for gobbling. There are hundreds and hundreds of thousands of them on loan by the week, the hour or for special outings to the seaside. They're usually sweet, reserved and quietly resigned to the one million nincompoops that swarm all over them – from the lackadaisical Americans, the wormy French and the *schlerping* Germans to the red-necked Australians with their foreign limbs too big for the tuk-tuks, their voices raised to 'Fuck you' level, their tables covered with half a dozen bottles of Mekong whisky.

I saw one scooter filled with four girls who were clustered around a really ugly non-person, wearing a big black pair of shorts and a sleeveless T-shirt. From my tuk-tuk I could see streams of raven hair swirling in the traffic and little hands tapping the pizza dough of his overhanging back. As we passed them, the man raised an arm to point at something and two of the girls took the opportunity to wiggle their fingers into his armpit, causing him to yelp, 'Hey hey, you little fuckers, don't be greedy! There's enough for all of you!'

Chapter Four

Foaming

At the end of the second week I had to go to the dreaded Medusa-like Department of Visas to whine and beg for a seldom-approved extension. I had been forewarned by the guidebooks that under no circumstances did they give you more than a week, three days being the average allotment. We needed a month: two weeks for Pierre to get out of bed and another two weeks to recuperate in the sun on the beach in Hua Hin.

My working attitude would be: *This is a State of Emergency, We Will Not Be Rushed. My Husband is a Legitimately Sick Tourist And You Must Show Exemplary Understanding Or I Will Cable My First Cousin at* The International Herald Tribune *And Thai Intransigence Will Be Smeared Across The Headlines.*

The sign at the entrance said:

NECESSARY FOR VISA EXTENSION

3 photographs
photocopy of airplane ticket (round trip)
passport
photocopy of present visa
photocopy of page 1 and 5 in passport
photocopy of any other documents
completed questionnaire signed by applicant
20 dollars fee per person per application
(no refund in case of refusal)

It was ten o'clock in the morning as I entered the small waiting room which was already overflowing with tourists milling, filling out forms and waiting for the next step. I waved myself an important passage and reached the application desk.

'Foam!' ordered a Noriega look-alike who was sucked hermetically into his military uniform, not a bulge or a fold or a dimple to be seen. He sported tasteful, streamlined epaulettes and what looked like a very expensive gold Swiss watch, although it could have been an imitation.

'I want a visa extension for my husband, myself and my child,' I demanded. 'He's in the Saint Louis Hospital after a heart attack so we cannot leave.'

I might as well have explained to him my method of ironing linen shirts with a slightly damp cloth, for all the understanding he showed.

'Foam!' he yelled again and held out his hand. When all he got was an American Bald Eagle stare, he shook his head sadly, reached into his desk and took out a sheet of paper.

'You write foam. You come back.'

'Three, please. We're *three*.'

'One, you one. Only for personal application.'

'My husband is *sick* and my daughter is *little*. I need two more for husband and baby.'

He lit up a Benson and Hedges, took a few drags, then reached back into his desk and handed me a second form.

'Could I have another one?' I asked blandly. It was getting time for a spelling of Mississippi. Some English tourists came up behind me with completed applications and the official tried to shoo me out of the way – but this was what I had been rehearsing for in the hotel mirror.

'Could I have another form, please?' I insisted. 'For my *baby!*'

The English couple, respectable pastel people, glanced at me curiously and then the officer looked at them and finally made the decision to save himself a lot of trouble. He gave me what I wanted, but I could tell by his eyes that if it had been up to him I'd be flying over Burma by now. I clutched the papers and ran off like a rabbit with a bunch of lettuce leaves. I was sure they would refuse; they would force me to leave within three days. We'd be forced to prise Pierre out of the hospital and persuade the French Embassy to send in a military plane to escort him out of the country.

Outside, a tuk-tuk gurgled up to me, blocking my path, and the driver, apropos of nothing, screamed 'Forty baht!'

'But you don't know where I'm going!' I exclaimed.

'Where you go?' he countered furiously.

His body was scrawny and he had a facial tick.

'Across the street,' I said, trying to pass in front of him.

'You come! You come! Inside, mister!'

He was like an irate dog owner trying to get a nervous animal back in the car. I stepped up my pace and just made it past the parking lot when I heard him reverse and then accelerate in my direction. He slowed alongside me with his head stuck out of the canopy, his eyes narrowed and his mouth twisted up. *Why is insanity my constant companion?* I asked myself.

We advanced, side by side, for some intense, karma-filled moments until a droopy German couple stopped him to ask how much it cost to go to the Crocodile farm.

This was instant revenge for my refusal, so he demanded a whopping 300 baht, which was practically half the price of a ticket to Singapore. When they naively accepted I was tempted to intervene, but upon examining their unisex, satin jogging shorts and tank tops printed with the symbols of male and female, my altruism evaporated. I figured that the Deutschmark was strong enough to bear the rip-off.

Back at the hospital, Pierre was sitting in a wheelchair surrounded by frangipani, hibiscus, breadfruit and Ava.

'Guess what?' she said. 'Daddy's got a girlfriend!'

Pierre peered up at me, benign and weak.

'Lots of girlfriends,' he corrected. 'They won't leave me alone! Four to wash me, two to comb my hair and two to wheel my tray! Today, the one with the ponytail said, "You are a beautiful husband" and gave me a chocolate. I love it here.'

I settled down to fill out the papers. The questions were predictably dull: mother's maiden name, exact time of entering Thailand, did we come by plane, train or boat? Answering these things three times produced sharp cramps of boredom in my fingers, but when I finally came upon an open question I was stumped: WHAT ARE YOUR REASONS FOR REQUESTING A NEW VISA? I could not decide on the voice or the right combination of pathos and determination. Should I just write 'heart attack' or would that look too flippant? Or should I explain individually – for Pierre: 'I have just suffered a heart attack and am currently being treated in the Saint Louis Hospital. I need time to terminate this treatment and then time to recuperate at a beach resort before the tiring ordeal of air travel.' (But 'beach resort' sounded like a slip). For me: 'My husband is sick and needs my constant attention. I cannot leave him alone in a foreign country, unassisted . . . ' (Would they be offended by my calling Thailand 'foreign'?) For Ava: 'My father is in the hospital and I can't leave my parents. I'm too little to travel alone. Please don't separate us!' The choice of correct plea was ticklish.

Armed with the 'foams', the photocopies, the passports, the doctor's certificate, the hospital certificate and the money, I attacked the Department of Visas the next day at half past eight: opening time.

The waiting room was empty and Noriega was alone behind his desk, drinking coffee and looking suddenly abused by my bushy-tailed arrival. He accepted my documents, flipped through them, sighed, stood up and was about to take them to the higher-uppers when he stopped. Pierre's and Ava's applications appeared under my nose.

'You write?' he asked, pointing to the questions.

'Well, yes. My husband is sick and my daughter doesn't write in English.'

He shut his eyes, not wanting to admit such haggling.

'You sign papers . . . self?'

'Mine, yes, but husband, he sign, and daughter, she sign.'

'Husband sick. He no sign.'

'Yes. He *did*!' I affirmed. 'He's permitted to sign one little signature and no more. You understand. His hand can do it, but it can't . . .'

I felt like I was reciting *Winnie the Pooh*. He must have had a sudden flash of Thai passivity because he bowed his head, straightened the papers and walked into the adjoining office. On returning, he handed back the medical certificate and said, 'Government doctor, room one hundred. You come back.'

I walked through the office around clusters of spotless military personnel. They were all sleek as eels at their desks and engaged in small, non-official personal activities. One man was arranging toothbrushes and toothpaste in a glass jar on his desk, making sure that the top was screwed on; a beautiful woman corporal was eating sticky rice; men with the insignia and bearing of generals huddled and exclaimed over a large cardboard box containing dozens of bottles of 'Glint' window spray, with the enthusiasm usually reserved for Frenchmen inspecting their Beaujolais Nouveau.

At the back of the building on the first floor I found a door on which was written, 'Room 100 – Immigration Medical Officer – Communicable Diseases – Venereal Station.'

Now I'm in luck, I thought. *With all these serious ravages they'll surely be relieved to sign for a pristine coronary.*

I went in and sat down on a long bench with half a dozen other aliens who were awaiting inspection. I know it was mean, but I felt like a high school girl who's been called to the principal's office because she's just won a scholarship, but has to wait outside while the truants are being reprimanded.

An hour later, when my turn came, I pushed open the door to meet the gaze of a tiny-featured, miniature of a doctor, white-frocked and smileless. He looked at me the way he would have scrutinised a faulty handbrake or a mysterious lump in his thigh. I sat down to present my case. The whole time I talked he never said a word, never blinked, never really inhaled, but kept rolling his ballpoint pen around and around in his fingers. He glanced at the doctor's letter, then he looked at my left ear, then at the lotus blossom calendar on the wall. Maybe this was the time that you offered the bribe.

'I give you ten days,' he said through little corn-shaped teeth. This was so different from what I had expected that I burst out laughing. I can only explain it as a moment of grace.

'It *has* to be a month,' I said on the tailwind of my laugh. 'It has to be time enough for him to get stronger. If you can't give me a month, I'll have to go to the French Consulate.'

'*I* can give you a month,' he argued. '*I* can give you six weeks.' He was raising the stakes all by himself.

This was delightful, like watching a successful soufflé rise and rise and rise.

'But I will give you a month,' he concluded, saving both our faces. *Oh well*, I thought, *soufflés always deflate a little when they hit the cool air.*

He shot me a 'watch this' grimace, placed the form ceremoniously before him, wrote down 'one month', signed it, stamped it, tore down an ear from the corner, then signed it again. He didn't say a word as I left or make the slightest gesture – it was as if he were waiting, frozen, for a deadly snake to slide out the door. But I didn't give a damn about word or gesture. I had my month.

That night, Ava and I celebrated by treating ourselves to a Thai cinema experience. The film was *Batteries Not Included*, another Spielberg 'pampers special'.

The cinema was located in the centre of town in a shopping complex about the size of Nebraska, where high-tech open-fronted shops blared out hard, inane techno and simultaneously projected strobe lights into the faces of shell-shocked customers.

A giant computer directory, upon which we had stumbled, informed us of the exact geographical location of the screens: Rama I, Rama II, Rama III, Rama IV and Rama V. Ours, Rama II, was packed with rich Thai teenagers who were balancing bags of popcorn, ice cream, cups of shrimp and dried beef, chocolate bars and quart containers of Fanta. They looked like consumer Shivas, clutching symbols from both East and West.

The rule was to buy your ticket or 'reservation' at the box office and then go and insert yourself into the waiting line. At some prearranged signal, the heavy upholstered doors swung open and the ingoing group charged head-on into the outgoing, like American football teams. Popcorn went flying into new-wave beehives, gossamer miniskirts were ripped like spiders' webs, gold jewellery twinkled in all directions. I held Ava around the waist, instructing her to kick and buck.

Once inside we tumbled into hygienic, sheet-covered armchairs and sat waiting through twenty thousand decibels of Tina Turner for the film to start. However, when the lights dimmed, Tina evaporated and a solemn organ recital wafted out, while on screen flashed home movies of the entire life of the 65-year-old king. We had to stand erect through his royal babyhood, his rambunctious infancy, his clever school years and his wondrous marriage. When the national anthem came to an end, we had to watch, cold turkey, clickety-clacking reels of royal princes and princesses, meetings with international statesmen, encounters with everyone from barefoot peasants to Sophia Loren and Robert Dole, and lots and lots of Buddhist business at shrines and temples and ordinations.

I liked this king well enough, partly because the people's adoration for him was infectious; his picture was omnipresent in hotel rooms, bars, coffee shops, tuk-tuks and kebab stands. Whenever he appeared on TV jobs were put on hold and everyone ran to the nearest set to love him. I also appreciated his particular charisma which was a heady mixture of studious saint and accomplished jazz musician. But it was so trying, standing to attention for this lengthy video salute. The physical aching was exacerbated by the presence, just two feet from our bottoms, of deep, comfortable maxi-relaxers.

The Thais, of course, were immobile, their heads raised towards the Light. There was a hushed quiet, a stillness of will which was uncanny when I thought of all the sweet wrappers and popcorn containers being held at bay. At last, in one photographic explosion of majestic flesh, brocade and diamonds, the ultimate image of King Bumipol appeared, and the audience went, 'Aaaaaaahh,' as if they'd just witnessed an elaborate fireworks display.

Sinking back into the seats again was like being sedated. It was so good.

It's not that I don't like Spielberg, I do enjoy being distracted from this particular world, but I'm too suspicious of his alchemy to be able to approve of anything he does. He produces these heart-rated pacifiers for American screengoers, all those credulous babies born in the fifties, who seemed to have been promised miracles at birth. Maybe it was that first trip to the moon, or could it have had something to do with the steady diet of Wonder Bread, Superman, Mars Bars and light drugs. Perhaps we never got over the birth of TV. If television, the unutterable visitation of all time, can happen to us, well what's to stop other super-duper phenomena from dropping by?

In any case, a good majority of Americans are out there in their back yards, waiting for the UFOs, the Second Coming, the Word, and whatever it turns out to be, they have been assured that, like the Olympic games, the Event will take place in the USA. Spielberg, the movie guru, is there, exhorting us, showing us the way to *marvel*. Come on.

The Thais adored the film. They screamed like people on roller-coasters as the ten inch alien spaceships swirled in through the window, and when the flying saucers hovered together to procreate, the audience stood and applauded; they yelled out sing-song insults at the villains, and some women sniffled when it looked as if the old people would really be evicted. Unfortunately something happened two-thirds of the way through, a directorial loss of energy. The ending was abrupt and anticlimactic.

When the light and the roaring music came on again, the Thais and I frowned in disappointment. We were out of fantasy and back in the flashing innards of a shopping megaplex.

Every day of the following week was divided between diligent hospital visiting (Pierre was jolly and improving rapidly, although our presence did tire him), sightseeing, lots of Buddhas, plus great reserves of snakes, crocodiles, scorpions and tarantulas for Ava's edification, and for many hours on end – voluptuous hotel wallowing.

At half past six in the morning, when the sun heaved itself up, Ava and I had already been in the pool for 20 minutes. Maybe it was because we'd never had access to one before, or perhaps we had to exhaust our worries and tension, but we worked that pool, we used it up. We had races; we improvised animals diving, bulls, kangaroos, monkeys; we sang '*Douce France*' while floating on our backs, not out of nostalgia, but because it was the only song we both knew the words to, and also, every time we did it, the hotel maids would stand by the edge of the pool and sway.

After the swim, we'd get dressed and go to the coffee shop for pancakes, pork soup, tea and the *Bangkok Post* which was an endless source of horror and amazement. I took note of daily reports of 23 more cholera cases in the Neanching province, 280 TB carriers in Bangkok alone, dengue eruption in the south, polio and meningitis warnings along the border. By the sound of these incessant reports, I got the impression that Thailand was one of Saddam Hussein's pantries for storing deadly bacilli. I would soon be distracted by the human interest stories on page three, anthropological rubies, thrown out for the picking:

'STREET SWEEPERS'S POPULARITY CONTEST'
'DUTCH HAND FOUND IN POONALONG STATION'
'HOTEL SLAVERY SERVICE UNVEILED'
'WOMAN GOES CRAZY, JUMPS OFF BUDDHA'

It got even better at the beginning of February when all these fantastic fillers were put on hold in order to get the St. Valentine's Day preparations under way. I believe the newspaper even added more pages to its normal format, just to be able to cover the massive correspondence, salutations, messages and wishes that this feast evoked. Valentine's Day in Thailand is like Easter in Jerusalem, it's the equivalent of Elvis Presley's birthday in Tupelo. It's a gift. For two whole weeks, large companies issued half page valentines dedicated to their clients; employees wrote in starry hosannas about oracular bosses; hotels vied for moneyed lovers, offering such enticements as:

Valentine Night Love Party Extravaganza With Champagne Supper, Orchids for the Ladies, Chinese Aphrodisiacs Upon Request. Midnight Vow Exchange In Candle Light With Live Harp.

On the tenth of February the *BP* opened its entire back page to the people:

> Tuy I love you more than last year – Sexy Chick

> Baisi and Jam – You are the most loving sons – Mother J.

> Wat – You've seen me at my best, and you've seen at my worst, but you've never seen me when I didn't love you – Ning

> To the best parents in the world, for all you've done to me. I'm your curly hair daughter. I am forever grateful – Silkie

> Ratchapurdy – I would like to kill for you love you so much. Tell me why? – Big Boy

The cardiologist discharged Pierre (much too soon as far as I was concerned), propping him up on wobbly ankles, filling his pockets with multicoloured sedatives, boosters, declenchers, whatever they were, and pointing him in the general direction of downtown Bangkok.

I arrived one morning to find him sitting on a bench in the corridor, swimming in his jeans and T-shirt, about ten kilos underweight, his cheeks somewhere behind his upper molars and looking for all the world like an Appalachian potato farmer in a Walker Evans photograph. He had been up early that morning, walking around, getting his legs back, peeping into the other circular wards and the wide open rooms. It was the first chance he had for sightseeing since he'd arrived. As we sat in front of the nurses' station waiting for pills and bills, he told me excitedly about his 'tour', as if he'd just come back from visiting the Karen tribes of the north.

'See that room over there?' He pointed. 'There's an old lady, about ninety, strung up by her hands and feet with pulleys. Her spine looks like a slingshot. What could be the matter with her?'

'Why don't you ask one of the nurses?' I suggested.

'I did,' he said, 'but I only got a sarcastic wink.'

'Maybe she's a Laotian prisoner,' I offered.

Thailand had been having skirmishes on the border for the last ten days, during which several dozen soldiers had been killed.

'That's how American GIs are always trussed up by the Viet Cong in the Hollywood Green Beret movies.'

'And the fights!' he continued. 'All these guys beaten up, pummelled! Their heads are like sausage pizzas! There's one whole ward *exclusively* for broken noses!'

'Come on . . .'

'It's true! Go and look if you don't believe me. They put them all together, four or five to a room, because they're all beaten up in the same way. Their families are there, dishing out ravioli and sticky rice. You'd think it was Woodstock! Everybody's smiling and lounging. I saw men whose eyes were slits, their noses squashed around their lips, and they're waving to me, laughing!'

'That's normal,' I said. 'Thailand is one big repository of Aquarians, astrological lilies of the field. They're all like Zsa Zsa Gabor, head in the clouds, *la vie en rose*.'

I was also an Aquarian, sharing my birthday with such comets as François Truffaut and Eva Braun.

In spite of his enthusiasm, the nurses insisted on pushing Pierre to the entrance in a wheelchair while I ran ahead to find a cab. I realised that it was 12 o'clock in the afternoon again, the sun on 'broil', and I hoped that the brief contact with it wouldn't be too suffocating for Pierre.

Naturally, once all of us and the luggage were piled in the taxi, it turned out to be the only one in Bangkok without air-conditioning. It was too late and too complicated to find another, so we had to drip for a half an hour of red lights, traffic pile-ups and the inevitable, misunderstood directions. I kept watching Pierre nervously, expecting him to keel over onto the driver's neck.

I had the awful understanding that I was in charge now. I was his hospital and *totally* responsible for a damaged organ. This was a terrible mistake, I thought, a gross miscalculation on the part of the doctor, to put him in my maladroit hands. But there, somewhere in the background, I could hear my Aquarian locomotive chugging along, repeating over and over, 'I think I can, I think I can . . .'

Chapter Five

Year of the Roasted Ear

'Sorry love,' said the Australian girl who looked and spoke like one of the fiends in *Mad Max*, 'but can you speak bloody English?'

In the drowning heat she was wearing itchy-looking, grease-covered denim overalls, a man's long-sleeved shirt, and a cotton vest covered with football insignia. Her badly hennaed hair was piled up like garbage over her left ear, and a copper penis earring dangled from the other. She was bent over at a 90-degree angle, like someone trying to sneak under a turnstile; this was because she carried a backpack the size of a standard doghouse on her shoulders. When I said 'yes', she shrugged off her gear, drew herself up to her real height, and then whistled to her two male counterparts who staggered over and plopped down their doghouses. These fellows had on mashed Crocodile Dundee hats that were sweat-stained and thoroughly unbeautiful.

We were standing in the middle of the Central Railway Station, surrounded by every race, creed and colour. I was suddenly overcome by the irrational fear that all of those three million travellers were watching us out of the corner of their eyes and thinking, 'Look at those *four* Australians!'

'Listen,' began the girl, extracting a map from one of the many zips on her vest, 'we want to go to this place here, see, Hua Hin. You see it?'

She pointed to the coastal town 200 kilometres from Bangkok, the pleasant Thai resort with 'hardly any foreign tourists' that *Asia on a Shoestring* so highly recommended. I too had come to buy tickets for Hua Hin, which was easily accessible and the ideal place for Pierre to try out his unfamiliar, convalescing heart.

'Well, them bloody buggers over there,' she glared at the ticket counter, 'they're trying to put something over, see? See, it says here eighty bloody baht, right here on this timetable here and those bastards they're telling me *two hundred*! Not bloody likely!'

She was bright with indignation and her heavy earring swung menacingly back and forth. If this were true, I marvelled at the temerity of the ticket agent: it was like trying to pull the rug out from under a Caterpillar tractor.

'I've got a mind to complain to Information,' said the more outraged of the boys. Foolishly, I took this for a joke and him for a fellow *farceur*, but a certain tightening of the jaw muscle alerted me to my mistake. I tried to bend my guttural laugh into a throaty disbelief.

'Surely they'll be in cahoots,' I said, mysteriously transported into my mother's vernacular. 'Let me go and see if I can't straighten this thing out.'

I hurried off, glad to be on my own again and ready to practise some *savoir faire*. I approached the counter and a perfectly sweet man with handsome features and very good English, asked me what he could do for me.

'I would like three tickets – two adults and one child – for Hua Hin, please. Is there a first class on this train?'

'Yes, of course,' he answered, taking out tickets and carbon paper. 'It's the same price for a child, first class: five hundred baht each.'

'And, um, how much is second class?'

'Second is two hundred baht, Missus.'

Dutifully, I pulled out the Australian's price brochure and asked, 'But why does this say eighty baht? Has there been an overnight 150 per cent increase?'

'But we are Company!' He corrected me with much vocal parenthesis, pointing to the encased photos of videos and velvet recliners and attendants with blue and white striped uniforms.

'Company is very expensive,' he told me, 'but if you want, you go Thai National Railways, it's too cheap, eighty baht, second class, yes.'

The problem neatly explained, I bought three 'Company' tickets. It sounded so evil, but I *wanted* them. I wanted easy. After checking departure time and facilities ('Do you serve cocktails?') I went back to report to the Australians.

'So,' I explained, 'you have to go across the hall to the Thai Railways counter, and there they sell eighty baht tickets. This office here is for 'Company', some kind of private independent train.'

They stared at me, understanding slow to reach the surface, but then they broke into grins, and a spaghetti and meatball kind of good fellowship engulfed us. One of the boys took out a pack of Winfields and passed it around. I don't usually smoke but I figured that this was the equivalent of sharing sheep's brains with Algerians – a rude *faux pas* if refused. After a few seconds of oral aerobics and smoke swirls from lips to nostrils, the girl narrowed her eyes and, looking at the tickets in my hand, asked me, 'So, where are you off to?'

'Well, you won't believe it,' I said, 'but I'm going to Hua Hin too.'

'Fair dinkum!' she exclaimed. 'When are you going, then?' She casually butted her ashes onto her friend's foot.

'Friday,' I confessed.

'Friday's when *we're* going. Hey! We'll be on the same train.'

I sensed a mild class struggle on the horizon and felt the defensive need to justify certain luxuries.

'Actually, under the circumstances, I have to go first class.'

Well, it was true! We would probably have been hitching if Pierre hadn't been stricken down like Job. Their collective reaction was a slackening of the mouth and eyes shifting from side to side, like policemen who just realise they've given a parking ticket to a city official.

'Posh, eh?' said the girl, who kept her eyes narrowed and fingered her earring roughly. I felt like saying to her, 'Would you please stop fiddling with that penis!'

Suddenly, the three of them reminded me of the gargoyles I'd seen on the top of Notre Dame, and I felt misunderstood. Like a rapidly threatening sky in an August heat wave, I darkened and swung out, with the scythe-like strokes of an adorable person pushed too far.

'What does "posh" mean?' I yelled. 'That my husband just had a heart attack, and that I've got to get him somewhere before he drops dead? You think he should sit on a wooden bench in a crowded compartment, just so we can all watch him gasp and struggle and gobble his nitroglycerine?'

I felt both good and bad after that outburst; I was letting off steam on unknown victims, sparing Ava and Pierre all my nervous backlash, but the look on the faces of the Australians was as bad as anything. They were mortified, and they had the mournful 'don't beat me' winces of very large, naughty hounds.

'Bloody oath, woman,' cried the girl, 'we didn't mean something! I was just kidding. What is he, an old man, is he?'

I had to appreciate them after that; this lot, with their sunburns and hobo faces and strawberry stubble looked like decrepit alley-cats next to Pierre's lean wolfishness.

'No, he's not an old man,' I objected, 'he's very young for a coronary. He looks like Sting. It was just a freak occurrence. The doctor prescribed first class. It's a prescription.'

I must have sounded completely unhinged because the Australians started waving their hands in pacifying gestures and one of them said, 'I'm hanging out for a beer. Hey, love, we'll shout you a beer, what about it?'

That sounded so friendly that I went into instant deflate, waited for them to re-hoist their gear and followed, light-backed, as they made for the nearest noodle and Singha shop.

Their names were Rhonda, Reg and Dave, from Kingary in the north of Queensland, a big peanut-growing district. They turned out to be much younger than they looked, shockingly so, and I thought that the peanut must be a tough crop to have affected them so much. They said they were having a lark before settling down – before digging their graves, it sounded like.

'Poor bloke!' commiserated the one called Dave – he was actually very nice, the way a lot of people I hate at first sight usually turn out to be.

'Hang on,' cried Rhonda, 'we could all go together! We could all take turns feeding him or something!'

'He's not a paraplegic,' I said. 'He's just like us, only he can't lift more than five kilos, he can't go up stairs, he can't smoke and he can't eat steak.'

'E's not like *me*, then, 'e isn't,' roared Reg, who was vaguely upset by the comparison.

'So, lemme get this right,' resumed Rhonda, 'we'll all be going on the same train, but in different compartments.'

'Something like that,' I agreed, 'anyway, we'll probably see you in Hua Hin, I think it's a rather small place.'

'Yeah,' she added, 'we could hang out there!'

Me, Rhonda, Ava, Pierre, Reg and Dave. Somehow it didn't have that ring of *cinéma vérité*.

'We can't really hang out,' I said. 'Pierre has to stay in bed most of the time.'

''is name's *Pierre*, is it?' asked Reg. He could have asked, ''is name's *Chocolate Eclair*, is it?' and sounded just as aggrieved.

I stood up, thanking them for the beers, and said we'd see each other around.

Outside, it had turned dark and I combed the underpass, where the cars arrived, for a cab. It would be one of the frequent Bangkok rush hours now, and with a beery headache I couldn't risk a tuk-tuk. A very fat, heaving man came running up to me, yelling, 'Taxchiii, Taxchiii?'

We haggled about a suitable fare, but quickly came to a compromise which I didn't quite understand the details of. Elbowing and bellying his way through groups of vagrants with raggedy parcels, he led me down the curb, zigzagging among the buses and delivery vans, and then around into a farther, isolated parking lot. I was mulling over the Australians, not paying much attention, until he held open the door of something pachydermic, indistinctly greyish, and battered. I had a couple of misgivings, but I didn't feel like listening to them, dismissing the driver as some kind of 'pirate operator'.

From the back the driver was rounded and indented like a pumpkin, wheezing asthmatically when he pulled the gear stick, and the gears wheezed in imitation as the car shuddered back and forth. We crawled guiltily away from the station, turning down a dark side street that was lined with mini shrines and souvenir Buddha outlets. For the first time in Bangkok we didn't cross any ten-lane avenues and as we got deeper and deeper into unlit neighbourhood, my pulse rate picked up considerably. *Why was I so stupid, so intellectually feeble?* I cursed myself, looking at my face in the rear-view mirror. The driver also kept glancing in the mirror, but I defiantly stared him down. It was no big victory – he pulled his head into his shoulders, *humphing* and playing with a grungy handkerchief.

It was uncomfortably hot and humid in the car, even at 7 o'clock in the evening, and we were driving far into a purple nowhere. I wasn't too worried at first; I figured that if we stopped in a deserted area, considering his age, around 55, and his condition, metastatic, I could probably beat him up. However, when we *did* stop on a street the only other beings were roosters, and the sewers were gurgling wide open. His profile merged with film memories of Akim Tamiroff and Sydney Greenstreet and my thighs went as cold as icicles. A horrible thought crossed my mind: what if he had a gang of kung fu sons, waiting in the shadows! I would never be able to handle *them*!

Then this ratty conniver rearranged his lumps and tissues so that he was turned sideways with an arm and a breast slung over the driver's seat. He leaned towards me and inquired, 'You go disco, lady? Very disco! Nice, some Thai dancers. Good happy, lady?'

'Whew!' I permitted myself to take a breath of relief and a second one for ammunition, then, bellowing as loud as my diaphragm could expand, I commanded, '*Sukhumvit Road! Now!*' and pounded my purse against the door.

This was nothing to him. It was like cigarette smoke blown into his ears, like the present lapsing silently into the past. He continued winningly, 'Good Thai food lady. This shop brother.'

I had had enough. I scrambled out of the back seat, wrestling with the wobbly door, and when I was finally standing straight, I slammed it and gave the car a kick with my flip-flopped foot. Then I turned and marched in the direction of the faraway towers and strobes. The car stayed silent in the shadows. What was he doing? What was he thinking? Would he run me down? Were his sons around the next bend? Or was he just at the end of his rope, overweight, in a broken-down old wreck, his last idea fizzled out? Maybe he was slumped over the steering wheel, haemorrhaging from stupidity.

By the time I got back to the centre, it was eight o'clock and the spaces between my toes were lacerated by the ruthless flip-flops. I had to walk, duck-like, on the outsides of my feet in order to avoid razor-sharp pains.

I finally found a proper cab with proper credentials and proper air-conditioning, and I didn't even ask 'How much?'

I was tired and gritty and angry. I tried to think of something to distract me from the present. I closed my eyes and was transported to the back seat of a silver limousine speeding through Beverley Hills, on my way to the Academy Awards. I had been nominated for best actress in the box office triumph *Monkeys in the Rain*, for my moving portrayal of a spunky, blind, American woman, the daughter of a southern missionary, who teaches in Asia. She's unwittingly caught up in a web of intrigue involving drug runs and the CIA.

The odds are overwhelmingly against her survival, but what the thugs don't know is that this girl was raised by a Chinese *amah*, adept in the occult. The girl, though blind, can derange at will, by mystical control: she can hypnotise with her staring green eyes and her other-worldly voice; she can paralyse the brain cells with certain obscure words. All she has to do is turn in the direction of her assailant, sniff and whisper, 'How much?' and the aggressor is gripped with a piercing migraine, and, screaming in agony, he writhes on the floor, while his brain slowly oozes from his charred ears. She falls in love with a handsome photographer who looks like Sting (although she wouldn't know that), and together they try to bring down the criminals. To complicate matters, the photographer has a bad heart, which means he can't take any stress or excitement, so the girl (whose name is Sunny, by the way) has her work cut out for her; zapping and hexing, paralysing, cauterising and lobotomising behind his back, in dark corners, and toilets, train stations, noodle stands . . .

When the taxi finally arrived at the hotel I made a beeline for the dining room where Pierre and Ava sat, fooling around with poached fish, cucumbers, radishes and other purities, many light years removed from cholesterol. I sank into a healing sofa cushion and immediately ordered a straight scotch. Pierre pushed his plate aside in disgust.

'I can't stand it any more! My French digestive tract needs sauces and patés. I don't care if I clog up! This food is like eating pages out of the Bible!' Then, glancing at my disarray, he asked, 'Where have you been, by the way? Was there that long a line at the station? I had to spend hours playing Pick-Up-Sticks!'

'Well, they're not *heavy*,' I said, taking a sip of my drink. 'That's a good game for you, you start with something light and work yourself up to the *Encyclopedia Britannica*.' I lowered my eyes and said importantly, 'I was hijacked.'

'Maman,' interrupted Ava, 'there's a man here with only one arm! When he dives in the pool, he goes like this with his arm and points it into the water and it works! I tried to do it but my other arm keeps coming back up. Daddy said he would tie it with my belt. You know where that belt is, huh?'

A dramatic event could never be awarded its full importance with this child around. Anyway, my announcement didn't seem to have much effect on them.

'Did you buy the tickets? Are we going to the beach?'

'Yup.'

On Friday morning we had to get two bags of clothes (big bags), two bags of books (heavy bags), one bag of toys (awkward bag), one bag of medication (little important bag), one bag of cameras (big, heavy, awkward and important bag) and ourselves across this literally and figuratively fucking city. What's more, we had to do it at its worst moment (the train left at 12:45), without losing anything, exhausting anyone, frightening anyone, without getting gypped by anyone, without spanking anyone and without crying, *s'il vous plaît*.

I went to find a taxi outside our compound and led the driver into the driveway, around the swimming pool and up to the entrance. Pierre took the bag of medicine, Ava strapped on her toys and I hoisted the rest onto my shoulders, hips, elbows and hands. The porters had all mysteriously disappeared, and when we went through the lobby, several Oriental businessmen cast admiring looks at Pierre and our arrangement.

We settled comfortably in the cab, which was reasonably cool for a change, and sat back for a last tour of Bangkok. Goodbye you Stygian underworld, you stinking labyrinth of prey and inglorious couples, and so many broken, old people selling pieces of metal or a few peanuts while Burbank estate agents photograph them artistically in between smorgasbords of little girls.

We stopped for a red light near a tuk-tuk whose fare was one spindly adolescent and no less than 40 frozen chickens next to him, under him, on his knees, on the floor. As we waited, the seconds of the ten-minute traffic halt ticked by to the pitter-patter of the melting birds; the heat of the late morning sun flushed out soft ice mixed with bloody juices which slid down the seat, under the shivering boy, and eventually dribbled out onto the hot tarmac.

The station was packed, paved with Chinese families, together with their warehouses, their businesses, their entire stock, and even their kitchen stoves. The multitude – the People they speak about in Scripture – prevented us from opening the car door. Could this be Chinese New Year by any chance? The one they'd been talking about for weeks, but that no-one could remember the exact date of?

'Oh. Tuesday, no, wait a minute, maybe it's Wednesday, or maybe it's Friday . . . '

How ignorant we had been. All we'd had to do was to buy our tickets, and the Chinese New Year would have fallen on the day they were valid for.

The task before me was Herculean: I had to force open the door of the taxi with all my body weight while squashing about three or four lady revellers at the same time; keep them squashed as I shoved Pierre and Ava out of the car; scream shrilly for one of the porters with their roller platforms; run around to the back to pull out the bag from the trunk; run back to the front to pay the driver, and all the while cuddle my purse close to my stomach so nobody would snatch it.

After this was accomplished, we shuffled through the crowd to the official porter station where I had to pay a couple of baht to a uniformed girl, who gave me three receipts. We were then allowed into the departure area, to wrestle our way through whole villages of kinsfolk who were punctuated every few yards by women station cleaners, mysteriously dressed in silk and sweeping little claustrophobic spaces no bigger than doilies.

It goes without saying that 'Company' was at the head of the train, all the way at the end of the track, about half a mile down the line. It could have been excellent, a fine experience: the bustle, the Orient, the array of food and toys and colours, but I looked at Pierre and my heart sank. He was soaked and his eyes had disappeared far behind his glasses. I knew by his crimson ears that something was wrong, that it was too much for him; his ears always turned dark red when he was upset. They were like little friendly animals perched up there, ready to signal at the first sign of trouble. I fought my way to his side.

'Just a few more carriages to go, Pierre. I can see the name already,' I said. 'Are you OK? Do you want to stop?'

He shook his head but leaned on my arm and we continued, more slowly now, wearily refusing hawkers that waved dried beef at us, stepping over parcels, pans of grilled chicken legs, racks of boiled eggs.

What we desperately needed at that moment was for two firecrackers to explode, one on the edge of the track and the other a few feet in front of Ava. I screamed the scream of childbirth, a tremendous, cathartic expulsion of poisonous gases. Ava jumped backwards, and her toy bag fell, scattering rubber crabs, playing cards, marbles and puzzle pieces at my feet. To my left, three middle-aged jerks were laughing themselves to death at our expense. Pierre had stopped and was carefully opening the little dark glass vial that held the awesome nitroglycerine tablets. He popped one into his mouth, closed his eyes, and got high. Ava picked up her toys. I spelled Mississippi a couple of times.

We managed to reach the 'Company' wagon where two affectionate hostesses met us at the steps, pulled up our luggage from the porter and arranged it over our seats, which were nestled in a little air-conditioned paradise amongst terry-clothed armchairs, overhead videos, jasmine hanging from the side window fixtures and three glasses of fresh, chilled orange juice.

In spite of our tribulations, we were still half an hour early. We lay back in our seats, letting 20 minutes of uninterrupted Nat King Cole wash out our anxiety and soothe us back to hope in the immediate future.

Even before the first purrings of the engine the video squiggled on, projecting eight identical images of Mel Brooks' *Spaceballs*. The only problem was that it was dubbed in Thai, with the original English hovering not too far off on the soundtrack. Ava however, was quite happy to re-re-dub it into French, having already seen this film in Athens. As fast as the words were spoken, she was there, like some precocious, simultaneous translator, to feed us one-liners and prize nonsense.

This was wonderful entertainment for about 15 minutes but it soon became a strain on the few nerve tendrils that we still had left: the excited Thai staccato, echoed in English and then in French, plus the noisy rhythm of the antics had Pierre and I rocking back and forth like bears in a zoo. We moved down to the reading section, leaving Ava to chuckle alone.

I had forgotten that there would be countryside and landscape to be marvelled at. This was palm tree country, which 'Company' engine, trotting along at 40 kilometres per hour, was giving us ample opportunity to explore. It was also my first jungle ever, a very orderly one at that – acres and acres of tropical forest, with neat little clearings for the occasional village compound of wooden houses on stilts, surrounded by dogs and children and smoking braziers and colourfully saronged men and women weaving in and out. Sometimes the jungle stopped abruptly, bowing to large plains of rice fields, where hunched, aquatic figures waded through hairy lakes. *Was rice really worth it?* I wondered as Pierre explained the double planting process. I suspected that this was a relatively stupid question but, staring out at the labourers, the difference between them and their water buffaloes wasn't that evident. I would definitely buy a rice handbook that would explain this crop. It had to be easier than it looked.

We read. We slept. Ava came down the aisle at one point, to announce that *Spaceballs* had ended and been followed by a video of 'killers: horrible men who kidnap little children and cut their mothers' throats while they watch. It's too scary to look at.'

We could hear the satisfied grunts and blood-curdling screams exploding in the distance.

At four-thirty, we pulled into Hua Hin. I don't know what I had been expecting, maybe a Bangkok in miniature, or an outpost of favellas, but *not* this: a nineteenth-century colonial station house, little fountains of lotus blossoms underneath bougainvillea and tiger-lilies, non-mechanical breezes whistling through the trees, a sizeable cat population poised on a white picket fence to greet us, and little cement statues in all the corners, half-goblin half-animal.

There was also a stillness that we had forgotten existed. I was so delighted that I swooped up our luggage like so many bags of crisps, only to be relieved of it a few seconds later by two English-speaking rickshaw drivers.

'Where you want to go, friends? You like nice room, not too much baht? How much baht you want?'

They gathered us up like laundry and divided our suitcases between their two bicycles. This was my first experience of being pulled along by an undernourished teenager who probably weighed less than I did – who certainly ate less – and who pumped feverishly, glancing back every few seconds to flash me a heartbreaking Unicef smile. Trailers from *A Passage to India* and *The Last Emperor* came to mind and a vision of a disapproving Gandhi rose up like the sacred Shroud of Turin, in the folds of the driver's damp cotton shirt.

But Hua Hin was tiny, and before I had time to unfurl my raggedy altruistic banner, we braked to a halt in front of a big white portico leading onto an open-air veranda lobby and surrounding garden. An entire family of personnel appeared to bow exuberant welcomes, then encouraging us, they lugged our things to the fantastic football field that was our room: about 60 square yards of tasteful newness, furnished with two imperial beds, a refrigerator, four armchairs, two desks, a coffee table, a vanity table, a wardrobe and all perfect, not chipping in the corners like in Greece or mildewed, as furniture can be in France.

When the friendly maids could finally be persuaded to leave, Pierre lined up his pills on the armoire before undressing and collapsing on the western region of the bed. I changed into my bathing suit and Ava jumped up and down on her own bed chanting, '*La vie est belle, la vie est belle!*'

Chapter Six

Donna Loves Luana

Our hotel was near the beach on the main street, where the few cars had to vie for space with the happy-go-lucky tricycle drivers. They swerved like swallows from left to right, executing loop-the-loops and dizzying zigzags for the benefit of their captive customers who, sizzling red from beach abuse and with their mouths *oohing* in mock fear, looked like live lobsters that had just hit the boiling water.

We made a slow crawl that first night in the manner of turtles labouring to the sea, only not on our bellies but *for* our bellies. The road was sandy and dry, lined with soup stands, barbecue grills, tables of green cookies, porcupines of ravishing kebabs, Coca-Cola-in-plastic-bag vendors, papaya and pineapple sculptors and coconut artists. There was a stand that had cast-iron pans with little semicircles into which egg whites were dropped for a minute or two and then prised out, forming a kind of miniature toasted flying saucer, grilled golden on the outside crust but hot and wispy in the centre. Pierre bought two bags full – no cholesterol in egg whites – but Ava and I agreed that, although they were definitely delicious, something wobbly happened to our stomach after a few bites.

The big treat for the holidaying Thais was the roasted chicken foot. These were individually tied with string to little lollipop sticks, giving off the mingled odours of scorched pepperoni sausage and cigarette butts left too long burning on the side of the table. Abstractly, I could see myself sucking on the toes, really enjoying cracking open the nails and chewing the delicate bumps. Concretely, we held back, intrigued with the idea but culturally incapable, especially Ava, who revered animal paws and feet.

'Where are they now?' she lamented. 'How can they walk, poor chickens?'

The entrance to the beach was an ornate wrought iron gate. There, strange peasants dressed in gypsy-fashion, barefoot and crusty, sat on high stools of different lengths and peered off into the distance, over the heads of the evening strollers. The sand they guarded was white sugar, spread as far as the eye could see, under swooping tamarinds and royal palms that stood in relief against the gnarled shadows of the jungle hills in the background.

Women and children waded in the water fully dressed, their sarongs and thin shirts floating like parachutes on the surface. This made them look so much more natural and integrated into the landscape than the tourists who were prancing around in strained bikinis and ugly one piece bathing suits.

The Thais were at ease, both in and out of the water, without having to go through unhappy transitions such as stripping down in front of a crowd, or sacrificing much-needed skin to the ever-demanding sun just for the sake of a dip, or the worst, emerging from the water, swimming costume dislodged and pubic hair run amok. I made a mental note to try and see if I could billow too.

We walked down to the port, where five-storey fishing boats puttered in at sundown, and watched the men form chains to unload crate after crate, ton after ton of crab, octopus, lobster and tuna. They sounded wild, hysterical, furious at the burden of abundance. The Gulf of Siam is so packed with fish that there's just not enough room inside the water or out. The men had no time to stop, no time to even catch their breath and when several dozen kilos fell onto the pier, nobody bothered to pick them up. Nobody cared.

Trucks squashed giant red snappers under their wheels and children jumped up and down on mussels as big as teacups to see who could crack open the most. Thrilled by this bounty we went to a dockside restaurant to order two lobsters for us and shrimp for Ava, soups and Singhas.

I noticed that all around us tables were filling up with 'Girls Who Must Eat' and 'Men Who Must Screw'. You could actually read on their faces that *Miami Vice* tropical living fantasy. All these soldiers, accountants, supermarket managers, paramedics and travel agents would eventually go back to Phoenix, Turin, Bonn, Marseille or Bristol to become stout citizens who would appear mysteriously knowing whenever the conversation came round to the opposite sex. I scowled at them but they just pushed their sunglasses up on their noses and chewed their gum.

When the lobsters arrived we had to put the beer and soup on the floor to make room for so much Crustacea. They had been cooked, cracked, unhinged and gently prodded so that all we had to do was inhale and the pieces would jump into our mouths. Ava's shrimps, which were as big as babies' elbows, had happily been peeled, beheaded and betailed to spare her any remorse.

It was a nice evening, maybe even wonderful, but I wouldn't let myself exult – something could so easily go wrong, somebody could keel over at the drop of an exclamation mark, dysentery was a sip of water away, we could all come down with seafood-induced hepatitis.

Going back to the hotel, we were faced – or rather *I* was faced – with an ethical dilemma: how many people can decently squeeze into a rickshaw? It was too far for Pierre to walk and Ava could easily fit in next to him in the tricycle without too much strain on the driver, but when all three of them tried to pull me up, I balked. How could this urchin pedal our family load? I desperately wanted to walk, but it soon became obvious that these moral niceties were better off left in Hyde Park or Washington peace marches, because the boy got angry, indignant, as if I'd insulted his competency. He got off his seat, came around to arrange Ava snugly into Pierre, then took hold of my arm to force me up. When I was finally all wrinkled in, against Ava and my will, Pierre tried to rationalise.

'It's an economic reality, you know. Whole families invade one bike and roll through town, you've seen them. These drivers are like athletes, look at their calves! To them it's like pulling produce, very large vegetables.'

No, it wasn't. It was like pulling pashas, sahibs and landlords. These men would die sooner than we would; they would rupture at 35 and be cremated with their tricycles. All because of us. We rode silently in the dark.

Several puny baht, it costs for two kilometres. Why didn't we just climb up on their backs, wrap our legs around their waists and pull their ears when we wanted to turn? Why the courtesy? Pierre took out a ten baht note. I produced two more.

'Ten baht,' said Pierre, handing him the money.

'No!' I yelled.

The driver opened his mouth to bargain and I wailed, 'Thirty! We're three people here.'

Silence and embarrassment. He slowly took the money, put his hands together and bowed. He didn't smile, nor did we. I didn't even feel good. I felt like a moron. But that was how it had to be.

'Inverse bargaining,' growled Pierre, 'I like that. It's a very quixotic addition to your personality. We may become popular here – when the hotel gives us the bill for two thousand baht, you'll push it away and refuse to pay a cent under three thousand five hundred.'

That was funny, but I stood my ground. 'I'll pay what I feel like paying. If the driver is a three hundred pound Sumo type, I might even haggle, but if I see signs of exhaustion, or too much sweat, or pulsing veins – well, he can just open my purse and dip in. And if he goes uphill, he gets double.'

'And downhill?'

'I haven't figured it out yet.'

At the hotel we sat outside on the veranda, sipping iced-tea while clouds of obsessed mosquitoes dived and then slipped from our Autan covered bodies. We were impregnable, but they kept up their campaign, scouting for that one vulnerable centimetre. A beautiful little girl with great black, almond-shaped eyes came around the corner to observe Ava. They started playing in sign language, and doing tricks for each other.

After a while, the 'Rest and Recreation' crowd drifted in, lingering in the lobby bar for a last bottle of Mekong, and swapping Hi-Fi anecdotes. Their Thai girlfriends were ever alert and reliable, not at all worried by the bloodshot eyes, or the sagging red skin, or the complacent belches of these sorry shmucks. One by one, the males stood up to call it a night, waving slightly like telephone poles in a high wind. They would grab their gals by the waist, or pull them up 'playfully' by the neck, and drag them back to their rooms, with a few leers to anyone in their path. Poor human sacrifices, to have such delicate bones and lie under slobs.

We were reading on the beach, in what was referred to as a 'room'– a territory composed of three lounge chairs, four beach umbrellas clustered together, and a squat rectangular table. They could be rented very cheaply by the day, a wise precaution if you didn't want to go back to the hotel with third degree burns. The sun did grotesque things to the pale-skinned imbeciles splaying themselves for hours on straw mats. First they turned pink, then red, then really red, and then a colour nobody could see – the sun's glare, screening its vengeance. When they turned up in the cafés and restaurants at night, the new hue was mercilessly revealed: the shade was 'old'. It was as if these people had deliberately got up in the morning, looked in the mirror and said, 'I think I'll get a little older today, get a little more respect around here.'

We weren't taking any chances. The direct heat was bad for Pierre, I had skin like litmus paper and Ava was terrified of the jellyfish that had just been caught (about 13 kilos of shimmering, transparent ectoplasm). She decided to stay put, deep in her chair, safe and sound behind Roald Dahl.

We'd been loafing like this for an hour when a very singular, middle-aged, saronged and straw-hatted Thai lady tiptoed up to my chair, slipped her arm through my sarong and squeezed my thigh. Hard. My eyes leaned out at the edge of their sockets.

I couldn't take it any more. There were women in Gary, Indiana, for example, that were librarians, with lives like clockwork, who never had a surprise that wasn't planned seasons in advance and here I was, once again singled out for cruel and unusual treatment.

'Pierre,' I said casually, with just a fraction of uneasiness.

'*Oui?*' he answered, not looking up from his book,

'*Please!*' I cried, standing and pushing her hand away at the same time. She leaned back and drew out a long, silver book, shoved it at me and started caressing my neck with her thumb in the same way Pierre did when he wanted me to come to bed. I grabbed the book. Books explained.

'Luana,' she mumbled. 'Mine name Luana. You from nice, beautiful lady, nice, nice.'

Unfortunately her arm was in the way, so I couldn't understand what was written on the cover. Was this some kind of love at first sight that overcame nationality, language, gender, just one of those things like *Death in Venice*? Pierre looked up from his book, shaking his head as if he'd changed his mind.

'No, no,' he said, 'not today, some other time.'

She acknowledged him with a curtsy but let me keep the book. I put on my glasses, sat back and opened it to the first page while Luana rocked back and forth on her haunches, humming and grabbing playfully at my ankles.

'This is the best thing that's happened to me in Thailand! I will never forget you, Luana!'
'I thought I was drowning in ecstasy.'
'I'm a new woman!'
'Luana's massages are totally wonderful.'
'She's got the touch!' '*Mon Dieu, que c'est bon!*'

A masseuse! Why didn't I make connections? This was exactly what I needed – physical aid, impersonal encouragement to take on the mass of worry that I carried around. I would be remoulded into a Gloria Steinham clone, I would be transformed into one of those radiant women who wrote books like *The Life of a Shooting Star – The Rare Disease of Baby Sharon.* I would become one of those steel rods who are never discouraged, who take on hell itself and come out victors.

'How much?' I asked.

Luana first gave a long, whispering speech, none of which was comprehensible. She had quite a large vocabulary, but nobody had ever suggested to her that some words go before others.

'Much can, not so to feel. . . like it. . . up, up, over foot. Very good down.'

She raised her ten fingers and flashed them seven times.

I lay down on my beach towel and offered up the bunches of walnuts and No. 2 nails that had been knotted into my joints for the last three weeks. Luana knelt over me, running her fingers haphazardly, like powerful spiders all over my skin. This, I thought, would be called 'Surface Awareness' in the States. Ava was peeping out from her book, her disapproval mixed with embarrassment and curiosity. Very few people were allowed access to the body of a mother – this was *her* hangout, where *she* pinched and tickled and manhandled. Also, several people were standing around, pretending not to watch, and this offended her sense of general anonymity, very important to an eight-year-old. But I could see her interest, *quand même*.

She might be able to learn something here, some new grabs and minor tortures to lay on me in my unpopular moments, some inventive thigh pulls that she hadn't thought of before. Luana terminated the overtures by strumming her toes' heavy bases on my soles and heels.

But it wasn't finished. As I lay marinating in pleasure, just another jellyfish washed up on the shore, slowly, slowly, some fingers went safari into my hair. They prodded for root, they believed in scalphood, they went for it! And the skull stood below, unaching for once, at peace with its ominous self. I imagined heavy cream so thick it would hang in mid-air, plopping down and oozing around my crown, my ears, my nape. It felt so magnificent that I just had to cry, first little squirts and then fully formed tides that burst through my lashes and sheeted my cheeks like cling film. So this was where all the tension was stored! I had thought it was shacked up in my stomach and higher intestines, but it was here on top, hidden away like dandruff where I couldn't get to it. Just before I fell asleep I heard Ava calling to Pierre, 'She's hurting Mummy – she's breaking her head!'

For lunch, we went to the covered market, a wonderland of lush vegetables, sacred fruit, intoxicated flowers, apoplectic vendors, and last but not least, assassinated, butchered animals as an art form and the baroque presentations of warm, raw organs in the nude. The only way to describe it is to jump right in without preamble and list everything in sight. It's like trying to detail the Indian subcontinent – people have lost their lives. There was all the food I'd ever known or read about and twice as much that I'd never heard of, except maybe in a Tolkien novel.

The category of chicken alone could have filled a Penguin pocket book: dead chickens, live chickens, half-dead chickens, anorexic chickens, chickens plastered in mud, chickens that looked like canaries, handicapped chickens with missing wings, chickens drinking coffee, deep-fried chicken heads, chicken feet in jelly, chicken arse kebabs, candied beaks, chicken liver necklaces, stacks of dried chicken skin like old parchment in a Buddhist temple, tubs of chicken heart floating in mint-green treacle.

Just as fascinating as the chicken were the fish, miracles of variety, half of them dead and the other 50 per cent gasping like telephone perverts. In certain corners it looked like someone had thrown a grenade: splattered innards, heads tossed all over the place like pom-poms, tails strung up like party fans and the floor covered with scales.

Further on, bowls of pickled stomach lining alternated with plates of sliced pig snouts, mounds of black edible tar and jars of dark orange worms. Should I even mention those perspiring blue vegetables that reeked of menstruation?

If this sounds like a guided tour of the exorcist's kitchen, don't be more than simply nauseated; these ingredients were purely for home cooking. No restaurant or snack bar offered us Spring Snout Rolls or Stuffed Duck Lungs. The closest we ever came to real earthy cooking was the addition of a few baked pigs' heads here and there in certain barbecue shacks on the beach, but I think they were more for decoration than actual hunger.

Chapter Seven

Sleazebags Under My Eyes

I could have slept for decades in the Thai afternoon, flat out like a starfish on the giant bed, the sun spraying angry lines on the opposite wall but kept at a distance by the closed blinds and low air-conditioning. When I finally woke up I could feel the scratch on my thumb turning red, swelling. I could sense the heat outside pushing against the building, looking for me.

There wasn't a thing in the room to suggest a foreign country, a tropical outpost, not an object that couldn't be found at Ikea or Habitat. What it did have was space – Thai consideration for the traveller with overloaded antennae. The woodwork was perfectly executed, sculpted as if by the carpenter Jesus himself. The plaster was as smooth as Kraft's Processed Cheese. There were no cracks on the wall to snag my glances, nor could I detect the slightest stray cement deposit or warped tile. It took eight giant steps to patter to the toilet, which was big enough to do gymnastics in, if you were so inclined. I could stretch out everywhere – it was like being a child.

The water gushed out of the extra large taps with filtered determination. The soap smelt of jasmine and honeysuckle. The towels were as thick as hairbrushes and the size of single sheets. It took twelve giant steps to return to the bed because I wanted to feel my feet on the floor.

In the evening we went to Fred's place next door, an open sided restaurant with batik tablecloths, American and Thai food and an inexhaustible supply of war videos. The list on the wall included *Rambo I* to *Rambo IV, Deer Hunter*, *Apocalypse Now*, *Platoon* and their gory imitations: German soldiers of fortune, Cuban legionnaires – a potpourri of worldwide macho causes. We came in on the tail-end of *Full Metal Jacket* and sat down among two dozen customers transfixed by bursting guts and agonising cries, twirling pork chops and barbecued ribs listlessly between their mouths and the screen.

On the perimeters of the restaurant in the fluttering shadows, little groups of Thai neighbours had gathered to watch this slaughter of beefy, jock soldiers who were not unlike the clientele. Everyone except Ava, Pierre and me, was getting enormous glandular satisfaction out of this Hollywood excess. We couldn't leave because this was the only place that served tuna sandwiches, which were the only thing Ava would eat. Already her bones were alarmingly visible and she grew lankier day by day. My obsession became to hear her swallow.

When the film ended, the volume of the diners – gnawers would be more exact, gnawing on bones, gnawing on corn cobs – increased. I could also hear forgettable remarks from the lost soul at the next table,

'Hey, lady, you got any sauce for this salad? Like Russian dressing?'

The guileless fool then mimed 'rush', pushing his elbows up and down and panting.

'*Rus-she-an*', he tried again with articulated loudness, the last resort of the exasperated American. He sat back looking forlornly at his plate which was heaped with dry sprouts, lettuce and mint leaves.

'Never mind honey, just give me some Thousand Island,' he drawled. The waitress brought him hot peppers and soy sauce.

I shifted around from this disturbance and my eyes caught the couple on our right, a matching pair of Napa Valley dolls with sun thrilled hair, necks gentled by white peach fuzz, those faces of sit-coms, reactionary tans mocking us and loosely clinging tank tops that casually revealed million dollar bodies. They were so self-conscious of their treasures that they couldn't carry it off; they posed, looking at uninteresting shelves on the wall with feigned intensity; he cracked his knuckles and said, 'Whew!'

She took out a pocket calculator and plunged into solitary, complicated, operations. What was she counting? Their calories? Their budget? How many good years she still had left? The compatibility of their genetic codes?

Other sorrier diners studied them obliquely, probably wondering at such unfair advantages. Aside from this couple, and Pierre and me, all the others were motley rejects, sitting proprietorially with 'Girls Who Must Eat'. From their point of view it might have looked like some terribly aesthetic god had decreed: 'From these same ribs shall spring like, but from *your* unhappy bones will be *nothing*! Go forth and *buy*!'

In mid tuna sandwich Ava saw her friend Na, the owner's daughter. They ran to each other in relief, to gesticulate and consult behind the counter. I heard bangings and thumps, followed by spurts of broken English. Then they ran over to the VCR and shoved in a cassette.

We all watched *Police Academy I* which was so dopey and hilarious that everybody ordered more beers to slake the thirst of laughing so much on a hot evening. Thais, Americans, French and Germans alike smiled and looked around, sharing a recognition of silliness. How we slalomed from morning to night.

At dawn the next day, I woke up and sneaked out alone to have breakfast and think, untroubled by family deterioration and undistracted by 'specimens'. I had to get some fresh insight in order to break down the emotional sediment that was accumulating daily, clogging my hope and blocking air to my morale.

I could feel panic gently lapping at my feet like the soggy shoreline of a polluted lake. I had to shake off these dastardly suppositions: what if Pierre dropped dead the next time a dog barked? What if Ava were perishing? What if we weren't taking the right dose of quinine? What if we got shot? This was one of the newer possibilities brought on by the discovery made the day before, that an unduly high number of Thai men carried guns tucked into their belts, their glove compartments, or in casual holsters. The police all had pistols bigger than their feet, dangling like swords on musketeers. Butor in his *Letters from Thailand* said that every man carried a gun and that it got very dangerous at weddings and ceremonies when everyone was drunk and started firing left and right.

Besides this, I had overheard people in restaurants talking about tourist beatings and eye gouging and I had read three or four inhuman interest stories in the newspapers about slaughtered Belgians, decapitated businessmen and bandit attacks on tourist buses in the countryside. One lady in the hotel said that the bus company had taken her picture before an excursion to Chiang Mai, so that in case of attack or ambush, they could identify the foreign corpses. If I had wanted to I could easily have whipped myself into a working hysteria.

No. I had to nip this cowardice in the bud. I had to appreciate a few facts. First of all, we were completely isolated – except for a Visa card and a few good books – in a foreign country, a *really* foreign country what's more, not your everyday Ireland or ho-hum Switzerland, without families or friends to act as buffers and comforters (those first aid contingents in life who rush in at the beginning of trouble with 5,000 true tales of horror that turned out OK in the end, so *don't worry*). I'm talking about those aunts and second-best friends, who scream out stories of their anorexic youth when they weighed eighty-two pounds at five foot nine and look at them today – size 42 D-cup.

There weren't even any booster magazines around to lull me into a domestic compromise with fate with articles like 'How to Cook for a Convalescent' or 'Cardiac Taboo: Sex and its Alternatives'. And there were probably tips, advice and recent developments that I wasn't being informed about. For all I knew, there could be revolutionary magnetic undershirts that turned from white to bright green at the first sweat of an oncoming attack. There were probably glorious gourmet artery-friendly diets that I was missing now that I most needed them. And the Surgeon's General latest report on child obesity and how it's imperative to under-nourish little girls. Of course I wouldn't have had any of these palliatives on a Greek island either, but there the *den perazi* attitude would have taken over, that eternal Hellenic reaction to bad news: 'Who cares?', and we would have believed all those convincing shoulders, shrugging away our fears.

What I had to do was fix on some kind of continuity. I had to set up an outlook that would connect us to the mainstream. We had to break out of this sinister air-bubble. But how? Maybe we should have made some friends, but so far there had been nobody except the Thais, whose non-grasp of English left little room for sociability, and the single-minded tourists who mostly looked like extras in a gorilla documentary. I mean, we weren't going to pour our hearts out to somebody wearing a 'MARRY ME, I'M FROM NEW JERSEY' T-shirt, were we?

The only thing I could think of was to make light, *toujours gai*, to soft-shoe through the day, to try for serendipity. I had to become a Lucille Ball type of woman waving a zany banner, otherwise we'd certainly slide into a morose universe of precaution, literal thinking and reactionism. We were too young to be old.

Feeling slightly better after breakfast I went out on the veranda for my morning fix of the *Bangkok Post*. It was truly a collection of the most quixotic journalism, the freakiest bulletins and most off-beat editorials that I had ever come across in my worldwide pursuit of inanity. A lot of it wasn't really the newspaper's fault but straight and faithful reporting of incidents conceived in hell and brought to stillbirth, usually in and around South East Asia. Ornate mutilations, Cecil B. De Mille massacres and brain-damaged dictators competed for space with stories of industrious lepers, Elton John's bowel history, the grotesque sex life of a woman rapist, Jane Fonda's exercise for flabby upper arms, and a recipe for monkey stew.

I had to get hold of this paper every morning and I would wander all over the hotel grounds if it were missing. It had me titillated to such a point that I was sure if I let a day go by, then *the* outrage of the millennium would take place and I wouldn't know about it.

I scanned the first page which was hogged by accounts of the Stock Market crisis, nothing very interesting really, unless you wanted to get excited about a small paragraph at the bottom of the page, concerning the forthcoming election of Miss Thai Thigh, a beauty contest for legs only. Beauty contests were very important events in Thailand, like bullfights in Spain – dramatic fire escapes from sizzling poverty. In the five weeks I was there I noted the Miss Bangkok Taxi Contest, Miss Word Processor, Miss Hostess of The Year, Miss Textile Queen and Miss Exciting Valentine.

It wasn't until the fifth page that I got the shock, that rush to the brain that imaginative exaggeration provokes. It was the report of a speech given by the Foreign Ministry Director of Economic Affairs who was calling on a visiting Japanese delegation to provide greater access for Thai goods.

'If Japan was a lady, she would be the original Iron Virgin, rejecting all attempts to penetrate her.'

In praising the continuing cooperation between Japan and Thailand over the years, the Director General said that:

'Japans suitors, like Thailand, had noticed a more relaxed approach and even a glimpse beneath her kimono, and this has convinced the suitors to choose the path of peacefully wooing the Iron Lady rather than attempting violent rape. The final objective for Thailand, the suitor and Japan, the maiden . . . should be benefits for both sides. Romancing a reluctant virgin is always exciting but it's more important that the final consummation prove satisfying to both parties concerned.'

Na was probably the most beautiful child in the world. Seven years old, she had straight chin-length hair, a tiny strawberry nose, and eyes you would usually only find on panthers or jaguars. Every time we went to her mother's restaurant, a tourist would be taking a picture of her. She and Ava started playing together, and before we knew it, every quarter of an hour, whether we were napping or dressing or doing lessons, there would be a slight scratching at the door. Since it was impossible to ask her to regulate her visits because of the language barrier and because we were only too glad for Ava to have a friend, we became resigned to waking up, or getting up, or dripping out at the first little noises from the threshold. She came in and usually sat in the corner, staring, until something enticed her into a babble of very idiosyncratic English. 'Vely mice, yes,' or 'Bad baby, I no you eat', or 'Me like boom, boom, boom.'

One day we took Na for a walk along the beach with us, and passing an ice cream vendor who only sold chocolate, I asked her and Ava if they wanted any. Na looked in the freezer, then wrinkled her nose and said softly, 'Chacola ice cream fuck you.'

My first thought was that maybe she was confusing 'fuck you' with 'thank you', but when I asked her again, she clearly didn't want it. Could it have been an insult to offer chocolate to a girl? The Thais did have some peculiar taboos like not pointing one's toes in the direction of another person. I also knew that there were different formulas for men and women, that even the word 'hello' changed according to the sex of the speaker. But she was laughing again and playing with Ava and a few of the freewheeling beach dogs, so I didn't think about it any more.

As we were walking back to the hotel, we passed a huddle of other black-haired children who were bending over a cat. Na pointed to them and pulled my skirt, saying severely, her beautiful eyes narrowed in disapproval, 'Thai baby, no good! Thai baby, fuck you!'

Then I understood: this particular usage meant 'I don't like.'

'Na,' I said, '"fuck you" no good, "fuck you" bad. "I don't like" good. "I don't like Thai children", good.'

God, I thought, *what am I doing, teaching her to be a racist in her own country?* She was already repeating,

'I doh like Thai baby.'

'I don't like chocolate,' I rectified.

'I don like chocolate,' she mimicked.

I picked up some dirt from the road, shook my head and threw it back down, shouting, 'I don't like!'

She laughed and said, 'I don't like Thai baby! I don't like chaclat! Fuck you!' All this so softly, like a cat swishing its tail.

Pulling Ava over, I tried a different tactic.

'We've got to teach her what she's saying or she's going to get in trouble one of these days. Now, you and I pretend to have a fight, to show her angry people, and then we yell, "Fuck you!" OK?'

'OK, Mummy,' she whispered conspiratorially, screwing her face into a snarl.

'Na, look!' I yelled as I pushed at Ava.

'Fuck you!' I roared, waving my fist.

'Fuck you!' bellowed Ava, giving a fine imitation of Harvey Keitel in *Mean Streets*.

Some passing tourists glanced at us, alarmed by this low-life exchange.

'You see, Na, "Fuck you", big fight, bad, no good. "I don't like." Good! "I don't like coffee. I don't like chocolate. I don't like bad man".'

She listened carefully and whispered, 'I don't like chocolate, I don't like bad man.' Clean.

'Good! Very good, Na!' I congratulated her.

When she came to our room that night, we offered her some pineapple at which she wrinkled up her nose and cutely showed off.

'I don't like.'

'Wonderful, Na! You're a smart baby.'

Two days later, we were in Fred's place eating our six hundredth tuna sandwich and watching *Over The Top*, another Stallone extravaganza, the perfectly worthless story of an international arm wrestling championship. Na was sitting at a table not far from us, puffing like a defective exhaust pipe on a long filter-tipped cigarette. I was just about to say something when her mother came out of the kitchen with a shriek, ran over and pulled the cigarette out of her mouth. She took Na by the shoulders and shook her back and forth, riddling her with recriminations. Na screamed and her mother slapped her face.

'Fuck you!' yelled Na.

I inspected my sliced pickles and tried to avoid Ava's accusing stare.

The Thai houses were dark wooden boxes on stilts possessing detachable panels that could be removed or added, according to the dictates of the weather. During the rainy season it appeared that people could wade from one building to another, climb up to the first floor and, by the time they got there, the heat would have already dried their bare feet and the bottom of their sarongs. At this time of year, life was said to have a slightly liquid quality, but nothing changed essentially. I didn't know at what point in the season, if ever, the walls of the houses were re-attached. It's always hot in Thailand and when it's not hot, that's because it's hotter.

It was interesting to see the social differences as mirrored in the local real estate because the architectural pattern itself was without variation. There was a single blueprint for several thousand houses, but the elite managed to distinguish themselves by darker, more expensive wood, more jungle attached to their property, and with modern furniture such as chairs, couches and beds with legs.

The less fortunate revealed their lack of ambition, or luck, by an irresponsible but winning unkemptness: all sorts of tropical weeds, clothes lines that took the place of floral landscaping, dozens of beaten up, rowdy dogs frolicking in rubbish which had been loosely tossed under the houses. Inside the rooms, people were lying on the floor, often sleeping, sometimes watching TVs that flashed at shin level in the corners.

A lot of inactivity went on in Thailand. Even in hectic Bangkok, one or two of the personnel in every shop were inevitably catching their 40 winks between the counter and the backroom or *on* the counter – in which case business was conducted over and around the curled up bodies. Observing the ease of Thai relaxation and the way they could nap anywhere, under any scrutiny, I thought about how little approval there was in the West for rest – or rather, conspicuous rest. You never saw, say, a Burger King counter person reclining under the cash register, or a secretary hunkered down next to her filing cabinet. I myself was a little embarrassed to be caught lying on the living room couch by anyone outside my immediate family.

What was nice about Hua Hin was that you could just wander around and look into all the houses, like in the 1940s films that went back in time to review the old homestead from the dark shadows of nostalgia. This visual permissiveness was a delicious slaking of my 30 years of closet voyeurism that had been restrained by the brick armouries of New York and the imposing stone farmhouses of Europe.

Ava and I strolled along the hibiscus-lined streets after dinner, gawking and marvelling at the spectacle of private life. Coming from America with its gerontological reservations, and France with its stockpile of lonely rich widows, it was delightful to be privy to the booming cult of ancestral veneration: every

house had its grandmother and grandfather, proudly
rolled into one corner or another, dry, noodled, billeted
and cosily propped up to watch the odd Thai game
shows, where contestants responded to complicated
geographical questions, only to be interrupted halfway
through their answers by bleatings, chirpings and
whistlings, which they had to imitate, all the while
retaining the solution to their original problem. From
time to time, the old people would wander out dazedly
to see the street and were they old! Transparent, sapless
skin hung loose from the bones of three generations
ago, while their chests twisted into crepe-like stomachs
that sank into sarongs and reappeared below,
transformed into sallow knotted calves and feet, very
similar to the mangled drainpipes in my Greek kitchen.

Once, we turned a dirt corner near the docks and
happened upon a crowd of elderly Siamese milling in
the dark, staring at three yowling housewives who were
staggering around their common yard, verbally
lacerating each other and aflame with unbearable
indignation. Ava and I sauntered over to the sidelines
where we had an excellent view of Sweetness
Debunked. The tiny Thai features, so practised in
courtesy and beauty, broke out of those faces like bats
streaking from a moonlit barn. I would *never* have
wanted anyone to come at me the way they were raging
at one another. There was no physical aggression – the
staccato dagger jabs of their insults made it unnecessary
– but the unleashed faces, three yards away, were the
mugs of hellhags, enough to haunt you forever.

The audience, though, was hardly intimidated. The
bystanders chortled, yelled out judgemental remarks,

and laughed together at certain savoury accusations. I had all the trouble in the world pulling Ava away. It was exactly like the Punch and Judy shows in the Tuileries Gardens in Paris, the stomping and caterwauling of costumed figures who approached the centre of the stage when it was their turn to denounce, and then retreated into the background as a new contender took the spotlight. It wasn't until the crowd got restless at the monotony of those repeated grievances and turned, one by one, towards us, and in particular towards Ava's startling crocodile cap, that she felt the urgent need to push on down the road.

I couldn't bear to see those couples any more. The terrible contrast of the 55-year-old, his body decaying in designer trusses, and a little girl next to him, 17 or 18, with her fragile shoulder bones and a single braid hanging down her back. The collective behaviour of these drakes and ganders, stags and billies varies according to temperament.

The Abashed or Guilty male keeps his slave at a distance, walking two or three yards in front of her until, by some kind of gravitational pull of the earth, she catches up with him and they admire the trinkets in a souvenir shop or briefly exchange a few words before he strides away once more. On the other hand, this conduct could be due to the difference in length between those vigorous, milk-fed, tennis playing legs of the buyer and the feeble limbs of a girl orphan.

Then you have the Clutchers and Gropers, usually younger than the first category and wildly excited by the great luck of suddenly finding themselves in the much heralded 'fast lane' – it's all they can do to keep from *vroom-vrooming* out loud. Their girls are pinched, kneaded, mangled, slurped, poked and generally devoured.

The most hypocritical though, are the Protectors, the salvationists, the gentlemen come to enlighten, not to violate. They do this by talking earnestly to their ladies, by teaching them the names of their 25 favourite ice cream flavours, by eating noodles fastidiously. They patiently explain the complexities of the *Rambo* plot in the video restaurants and refuse to order the girls a second round of beer, calling for fresh orange juice instead. They're adorable!

Everywhere I turned: sleazebags. But I promised myself that I would only write about the humanly describable. I won't even think of wasting anthropological commentary on most of the abominations. For example the burly, syphilitic-looking German, with that prickly crew- cut sticking up from his sour head and his size XXXL T-shirt depicting a lumpy machine gun underneath the stencil: 'Uzi Does It Best'. Nor will I mention the frail hummingbird who was with him, a black-haired Mia Farrow type, whose fingers were thinner than Marlboros and whose feet didn't reach the floor.

A few days later we opted for the flashier, more luxurious Silom Hotel, a few kilometres down the beach. Although it was hardly in our budget, we were having technical problems that necessitated a more wanton attitude concerning finances. Firstly, the water on the public beach had become glazed with very sheer creamy bubbles, strange plastic dots and tiny dead fish.

Secondly, it was too far for Pierre to walk the 500 metres to the seaside and when he finally got there, the massage ladies continually harassed him. They sensed the gross tension in him and approached every 15 minutes, shoving testimonies in his face and singing Beatles songs in his ears. Thirdly, Ava was nervously on the look out for jellyfish and finally, I was always miserably aware of all the indentured baby-women rubbing coconut oil on freckled white bodies that would have been much better off hidden away inside beige polyester leisure suits.

After checking out several billboard ads, Ava and I took a rickshaw over to inspect the Silom. It was on a private compound, set off from the main road by a gate and a winding driveway that led to shady grounds, impeccable lawns, an open-air teak veranda, scattered green Buddhas, parrots, and a large, brimming, twinkling swimming pool. A room on the patio was $30 a day – could it be bigger than the one we already had? It was seriously carpeted and boasted a bar, cable TV and a bathroom where two people could conduct their business without ever running into each other. When we went back to the desk to register, the receptionist took our passports, started to jot down numbers and dates but got confused with the hodgepodge of our nationalities and finally looked up at me and asked, 'Why were you born?'

Tricky question.

Chapter Eight

How Many Dutchmen Does It Take To Change A Sikh?

'I vas yoost a young mother, the year Corinne vas borned. I vas very tired, so my husband said to me, "Let's go to Thailand", so ve left the baby vit my mother and came to Pattaya for a month. It vas a beautiful vacation, and ve had a vonderful time, very nice, but on the last day I felt like a cramp in my bones and I think this is from sitting such a long time in my deckchair. So I vent for a valk but I still couldn't lose the cramps. Then ve had to fly home and I'm usually afraid, but this time I yoost didn't care, this time I vas so tired and pained that I slept through the whole trip and had no memories of changing planes in Amsterdam.

'Ven ve arrived in the night in Stockholm, I could barely valk, and ven ve got to our home I started to cry. I couldn't lie down on the bed, the pains vere so tirrible so my husband called a doctor who vud come in the night, and this man said, "Vere are you coming from, exactly? Vat! Thailand, a place vit so many illnesses! I von't touch you, who knows vat it can be!"

'Then my husband telephoned for an ambulance that brought me to the hospital and the doctors said "Yah, this vas polio"! I vas in hospital for six months.'

'But, hadn't you had shots . . . vaccinations?'

'Oh, sure. Everything I had before the trip . . . but it vas the strain, you see.'

'The strain?'

'Yes, the type, the kind. You have protection if you are vaccinated in Europe, against the European polio, but this vas very far avay, vas Asiatic strain, two different sicknesses.'

We were lying, wet, in the late afternoon shade, beside the pool, watching the children play the animal diving game. Corinne waddled, flapped, quacked and hopped into the crystal blue water. Ava crawled along the diving board on all fours, mooing and chewing until she sank off the edge. The movements of the girls continued rhythmically in time with the sing-song narration of the Swedish mother. On a greyer day and with a more allegorical story, it could have been a Bergman sequence.

'But don't vorry,' she patted me on the wrist, 'it vas only bad luck. Anything can happen anyvere. You think you're safe in Europe? My good friend in Stockholm, she's a lawyer, she's never left Sveden in her life. Von day she came home from verk – and her fingernails fell off! Yoost bad luck! Don't vorry too much.'

I closed my eyes and tried to squeeze one more fearsome possibility into the bulging sack of phobias that I had been carrying around lately. Shit. Polio. So familiar sounding, jocular even, and so ugly. I knew that from now on, every time Ava mentioned a mysterious pain, I would freeze. I quickly opened my eyes. A cute little 30-year-old nouveau riche Swissess came bouncing up to us asking, 'Have you seen Papa? Bébé wants to have his nap and he must have a kiss from his Papa.'

This was delivered in a rhetorical fashion, no response demanded. The speaker immediately pranced off, satisfied with her afternoon social exchange.

There's a different kind of fish in this Silom than the pissant Romeos of the other hotel. Here, there are either families or hearty, long lasting, elderly North European couples, out for a spin on their pension money, enjoying the last bits of elasticity, trying to remember what flirtation was all about but finding the stakes hardly worth the effort. They arrive by the busload in the morning and come down to lunch in energetic, rose garden dresses and Hawaiian sports shirts, stretched over vast fields of breast, ass and belly.

This is an extra-large wurst-worsted society, whose members, after decades of industrious excess, have taken on the protective coloration of beer barrels, pickled briskets, strudels and wiener mounds – kitchy, humanoid souvenirs of Fasching festivals and Bruegelian reunions. I can also recognise a lot of pre-cancerous skin here, once again that 'non colour', all the more chilling under the unwise Isabelle Rossellini-Lancôme make-up schemes.

As I waited for Pierre and Ava to join me, I was conscious only of pouches. I saw mumps and bumps and anarchic undulations rippling beneath flourescent synthetic material. Theoretically, breasts should be but two protuberances at their station on the human chest, but wherever I looked I saw Plutonian variations, three or four bulges where breasts are traditionally parked. And the women and men alike must have been doing villainous, heinous things for a very long time to have ended up with those sallow jowls and waxy wattles that dip towards martinis.

The hues that hang over the ocean and behind the very fat moon are so purple and black that they transform the whole *landscape into a tacky painting on velvet. A confederation of roomy hostess gowns shuffle onto the terrace, displacing many cubic meters of fragrant night air. I order and instantaneously receive another Bourbon, and when I'm just reaching the first solid footing of anaesthesia, a Thai rock combo whispers itself sideways into an introverted, mewling, dead-on imitation of Simon and Garfunkel doing 'Bridge Over Troubled Water'. Serving girls appear in sarongs and silk blouses, floating among the customers like lily pads in a hippo pond. The only thing is, they don't serve (the 'boys' are for that), they've come to talk baby talk to the, now, totally enchanted burghers. 'What your name? Friedrich? Fried Rick? Fried Rice? Tee Hee Hee Hee.'*

'Yah, Friched Reich! Hawf! Hawf! Hawf! Gut!'

The girls jiggle ears and squeeze already overloaded bladders, the wives put emphatic arms around the lovely draped waists and the whole world giggles shrilly in a sporty imitation of euphoria.

Two tables down, a couple is sitting next to the balcony with their backs to me – the wife on the outside. A Thai Tinkerbell comes to their table with a bottle of wine and pours it very slowly in the long stemmed glasses. When she finishes, the Frau customer reaches up to examine a little silver chain around the waitress's neck. While she's thus distracted, the husband, who is on the inside, slithers his arm behind his wife's back, grabs the girl's fingers and starts to rub them back and forth. The man's hand is as serious and desperate as a bear's claw grasping for a fish while the tanned fingers of the girl are liquid, evasive and finally, still. I keep looking for some derision in that frail arm, but I see only submission to a buyer's market.

When the singers launch into a pathetic attempt at 'Hey, Mr. Tambourine Man', there's an undercurrent of mnemonic stirring, some knee-jerk reaction to the memories of the bohemian, student prince years that forces up the noise level. They toast amidst cackles and hearty 'Yahs'. My cuttlefish rosettes arrive, snuggled down in a nest of basil.

Although the doctor firmly proscribed any sexual activity, Pierre's post-coronary depression provokes him into seeking life-giving activities. Since we go to bed rather early, the nights are long. We both toss relentlessly until exactly three o'clock in the morning when we very often find ourselves reverting to pre-coronary sensuality, which I go along with up to a point, but then halt, like a neurotic soap opera heroine for fear of a fate too evil to name. I eventually suggest that we indulge in some imaginative, albeit, pianissimo foreplay, but that at the ultimate moment I tell him a joke, so this way he can laugh and slough off the tension.

'Are you serious?' he complains. 'Don't you know anything about the male body?'

'But the doctor said it would be good for you to laugh! It's practically the same kind of explosion, the same process. You'd be doing yourself a favour.'

'Well,' he warns, 'it will have to be a really good joke.'

The next day the Sikhs arrived to set the Silom on its ear. They were a severely extended family unit, consisting of two brother-husband-chiefs, two or four wives, or two wives and two sisters, six children, one grandmother, one 20-year-old simpleton and three Thai slaves. They sailed around as One, and even when they spread out into groups of men here and women there, you could still feel the powerful twang of the invisible chords that joined them.

Physically (except for the servants), they were extraordinarily well-fed, but unlike the older Nordic packages, these bodies were firm and correctly rounded, according to the rules of biology – and a little more – for the sake of seduction. The women were the colour of walnuts and fruity, their adipose density dictated by the requirements of the *Kama Sutra*. Long black braids the size of swing ropes hung down to their waists, bouncing against strained, silver and fuchsia saris. The men pushed forward little rounded bellies as taut as basketballs, which they kept tightly buttoned behind silk shirts and they wore coordinated turbans that swooped up in front like prows. The children, spoiled and happy to be, were folded into creations reminiscent of meringues, maraschinos, banana splits and peach melba. They roughhoused in ruffles, taffeta, mesh and a little gauze in the evenings. These kids were straight out of Birthdayland, where every day was full of treats, presents and mocha sandwiches.

The first day, they raided the hotel gift shop and came in to lunch dangling silk purses, chains of silver elephants, papier maché bracelets and satin fans. I didn't know who they were or where they came from but they were certainly *chosen*, the radiant adherents of that swell philosophy: Valhalla Now!

Since the Sikhs cannot comply with at least two of the hotel's regulations concerning the swimming pool – 'It is strictly forbidden to swim in saris', 'It is strictly forbidden to eat and drink in the pool' – they have to eschew this luxury. In retaliation they monopolise about 30 yards of hotel beach front.

Mesmerised by their sumptuous presentation, by their train, Ava and I also casually wander down to the sea every morning and late afternoon, to lie near them and gather up the tiniest details of their extravaganza. They install themselves by joining together an infinite number of lounge chairs, umbrellas, cushions and tables to form a kind of ballroom so close to the sea that several ringed toes can be noticed flashing in the surf. After a quarter of an hour of urgent chattering, the women, clad in third or fourth best saris, rise up in a flutter and, forming a circle, they clutch hands and wade into the water up to their collarbones. When they reach this certain level after splashing each other and whooping and checking to see if their make-up is running, they suddenly quieten down and, all faces pointed toward the horizon, they begin to sing.

Then Ava and I can stand it no longer – we swim out to be near them, to lap up this beauty, this harmony, these lady dolphins in their shiny wet colours. They bob and trill and bob and chant. As I turn around to avoid a wave, I see other, older spectators, gelatinous, lodged in their deckchairs like Yorkshire puddings in their moulds, glumly surveying us.

'I wish I were Sikh,' says Ava.

'Me too,' I agree. How relaxing it would be to become part of their entourage; no more money problems, Ava would be fattened like a goose, Pierre's heart would be pampered by sweet luxuries of sight and sound, and even if he didn't survive, at least he would be assured of a fun cremation.

Now, it's Mekong whisky time for the chiefs and stuffed chicken leg time for the ladies. With voluble, detailed instructions, they send the slaves off for refreshment. They fidget in anticipation, they draw up closer to the tables, to be ready, and when the snacks arrive – two half-litre bottles of orange

alcohol and three platters of legs – they applaud with all their
hearts, in third world appreciation of answered appetites.

Alas, as in any romantic tale comes the evil counterpoint:
the rubbish goes overboard, greasy napkins fly through the air,
over the sand and onto the unsympathetic thighs of a shopkeeper
from Utrecht. Cartilage and fat are chucked into the foamy
water. There's a lot of gusty spitting going on, so profligate
that I laugh; it reminds me of a drunken wedding party. But,
consider the chagrin of these Dutch grandmothers who've spent
their whole lives eating Gouda off blue tiled floors and
disinfecting their windowsills. They launch hoarse cries of
resentment, but the Sikhs are in full swing, laughing,
munching, slurping, teasing. They heed nothing but their own
luck in life.

We waited at the hotel while Pierre took the train up
to Bangkok after his two-week rest period. The doctor
said his heart was back to normal. No scar tissue. He
could travel. Lightly. What did 'lightly' mean? I
imagined Fred Astaire in *Flying Down To Rio*. I couldn't
understand how he could have changed from a
doddering invalid into a tap-dancing wayfarer in a few
weeks' time, but again I wasn't asked.

'We're going to Malaysia,' he informed me upon his
return. 'We're getting out of these dry-cleaned hotels
and into the 'bush'. Five dollars a night, OK? You don't
have to answer, you have no choice.'

How could I tell him that what I really wanted to do
was to rush to Paris, check him into the best and biggest
heart clinic, drop Ava off at her cousin's in the country,
buy an angora sweater, stuff myself with green

vegetables, then collapse for six hours at a John Cassavetes Retrospective? I couldn't find the right words – so I just gave in.

Chapter Nine

Why We Didn't Go to Singapore

We took the night train from Hua Hin to Butterworth, across the border in Malaysia. We found ourselves, without warning, in a second class dormitory which had swing-up bunk beds and sexy railway box curtains that suggested immediate intimacy with our fellow passengers. We were in a compartment full of Polish backpackers, whose blind-looking, light blue eyes and ash-blond hair contributed much to the confusion I felt. Once I began to panic, stopping in mid-charade game with Ava, to scream, 'Where are we? What are we doing?' into the deaf Eustachian tube which was our purpose. Who *were* all these Europeans, alive and robust, and flaunting it? I liked Poles per se, but what were they doing eating cheese and tomato sandwiches on *my* mysterious journey through the Eastern night?

Fortunately, a commanding gong rang out from a loudspeaker to summon us into an Orson Welles thriller: a rickety food place with plastic chairs, stained cotton tablecloths and little glasses full of fat toothpicks. Two waiters ran crazily up and down the wagon as if they'd been stung by wasps. They screamed and gesticulated and rolled their eyeballs in kaleidoscopic formations like Japanese stockbrokers trying to make a killing. We ordered rice, broccoli, duck and whisky, which all appeared quickly before us. The train bounced, the waiters see-sawed, the whisky splashed – I felt like John Belushi streaking towards Chicago, jiving with a wired-up lunatic entourage.

Within minutes, Pierre and I were perfectly drunk and laughing like woodpeckers.

A Thai family – mother, grandmother, daughter – came in, sat down across the aisle from us, and ordered a meal. Ava made eye contact with the little girl so it was only a matter of minutes before we adults developed that benign facial morse of parental complicity. Ava, encouraged by so much good fellowship and inspired by our own mounting silliness, pantomimed a dog with its paws in the air, putting her nose in the plate to lap up the rice. When the other girl started to laugh and tap her fork, Ava sang 'How Much Is That Doggie In The Window?' in a very Maurice Chevalier accent. As she was singing, a tattooed Cockney suddenly lunged through the door, weaved his way up to our neighbours' table and mumbled in a *Clockwork Orange* drawl, 'Gimmie the fookin' kid, May!'

He made an abortive grab for the child who went to meet him with outstretched arms while her mother tried to jerk her away from the jerk. Then the grandmother started berating the mother and the little girl tried to imitate Ava imitating a dog and the Cockney looked over at Pierre for some male solidarity. Things began to get out of hand.

We paid as fast as we could and left. Were these goddam tourists *fathering* on top of everything else?

Ava woke me four times in that long night: twice to vomit, once to have urgent diarrhoea, and once to vomit and have urgent diarrhoea at the same time. Each trip to the bathroom called for double-jointed contortions in order to shimmy through the turnstile of hairy arms that were flung out through the curtains – but they distracted Ava and got her safely to the toilet, where the nightmarish tint of the evening was accentuated by the metallic neon lighting that turned her face from ash to green to a relatively optimistic chalk white.

I dug my fingernails into the palms of my hands and promised to keep cool. I would *not* do anything undignified, like sobbing or calling out to the Sacred Heart of Jesus in a Pavlovian throwback to high-school training. What I would do was flush the toilet, and if I could get her dressed and out of the door of the stall before the swirling stopped, well, that would mean that everything was going to be OK.

The following morning we were barked awake by a conscientious cabin boy who drew back our curtains and pulled us out of bed, re-establishing our bunks into seats before the sun even appeared over the rice paddies. After an hour of shuffling possessions, pushing for space and washing three to a basin, we were served the world's most inferior breakfast: two pieces of ugly, fungus bread and three cups of diesel flavoured coffee. Poor Ava, caved in from the night's vomiting, stared apathetically at this slop and said, 'Never mind, I'll eat an apple.'

I wanted to die of unworthiness. This child should have been having oatmeal and honey, she should have been playing Frisbee on a freshly mown lawn. I stared out of the window at the swamp we were passing and imagined one of the toads on the lily pads jumping through the curtains and offering me one single wish.

'Please,' I would beg, 'please, give this little French girl a fresh croissant and a big bowl of hot chocolate.'

Pierre came back from his morning wash, diminished and pale, with dark Italian shadows under his eyes. He sat down next to Ava and they became father and daughter twin sets of despair.

When we reached the border the sun was higher and the night's miseries were beginning to dissipate. We had more of a handle on the day, especially when yoghurt, tandoori lamb, gingercakes, sticky rice and Cokes started to bob past our windows. While Pierre got off to present our passports, I arranged our bags for inspection. According to the guidebook, this was a notorious drug pass and the customs police zealous in their methods. I inventoried our growing bag of pharmaceuticals: antibiotics, suppositories, sleeping pills, heart modifiers, tranquillisers, nitroglycerine . . . trying to imagine what the guards would make of them. I waited while the inspector did the blasé Poles who kept up their long running card game all through the check. I guessed that they were probably used to a much heavier regimes, next to which the Malaysian police were lightweights. I tried to pick up some attitude from them.

When it was my turn, the deferent young man approached with a bow and asked me to open my bags, indicating my purse to start with. This was something I had overlooked: the absolute chaos of my tote bag; the discarded Kleenex; the Lego pieces; about 70 Visa receipts; orange peel; a mummified chicken leg inside an empty Tampax box; a spoon; crushed almond biscuits; egg shells, iodine . . . all on the first layer. But this turned out to be a break; he seemed to realise that my preoccupations, as represented in my purse, were counter-indicative to 'horse' smuggling. Rather disgusted by his initial efforts, he just goosed the other bags, imagining, I supposed, monstrosities of larger flotsam and was turning away, when he stopped and twisted back in my direction, a vital point remembered. He put his arms behind his stiff uniform and stared past me out the window. 'Are you a Christian or a Jew or a nothing?' he asked. The 'C' of this multiple choice was spat out with such contempt that I actually winced in recognition but I managed to yell back, 'Christian!' with all the fervour of a *Playboy* centrefold.

'So,' he continued, 'what then, is the difference between a Christian and a Muslim?'

But I was ready for him there: I had been a *Time Magazine* subscriber for at least ten years.

'One has Jesus and the other has Mohammed,' I answered right off the bat.

He looked at me with cautious admiration, then patted Ava on the head; we were good guys, part of the International Sheephood. Of course, we would graze among brothers.

I looked out the window for Pierre and saw all of upstate New York standing on the platform: college dropouts, football players, Shriners, Hell's Angels – every single one of them was there, brandishing passports, adjusting earphones, chewing Juicy Fruit.

What surprised me the most was the number of 55 to 60-year-old women, tired but game. Half-matron, half-hippy, out for a laugh. I liked them.

An hour and a half later, we reached Butterworth. From the train station, it looked like a wasteland of petrol tanks as far as the eye could see. The real point of interest was Penang, a short ferry ride away. We got down and I popped veins transporting our weighty luggage across the tracks and through the endless terminal. Pierre was ahead, worried by the uneven distribution, but trying to be useful by locating the ticket office and entrance gate to the next ferry line. Ava was lagging behind underneath her backpack of toys and books. I saw her begin to swerve and her mouth open for no reason at all. The passageway was brutally hot with a stench of exhaust fumes and frying oil. The lack of sleep, the physical struggle and the pressure to keep us whole was suddenly overwhelming.

'Pierre!' I screamed, dropping the bags and grabbing Ava just as she swooned into my stomach. When I looked up, he was leaning against a cement pillar, shaking another nitro' into his hand.

'We've got to *stop* this! Slow down! Where are you running to? Your funeral? Is that it? I feel like a piece of meat in a tragic, tragic sandwich. I want to go back to Greece. I want Ava to eat some stuffed tomatoes.'

I had certainly lost my mind to tension and all I could do was sit on the luggage and cry. Pierre, alarmed, tried to buy a bottle of water but they only sold Cokes. He got a couple of these and some chocolate biscuits. We hunched over them like cavemen, pushed back straggling, soppy hair and mechanically stuffed our emotions with junk food. We were barely alive.

By the time we came to our senses again, the terminal was packed with hundreds or thousands or millions of dazed human beings pushing at the gates. We forced ourselves in with a fear born of surging insecurity: Pierre drilled a path, I thwacked people half my size with the bags and Ava, goat-like, butted with her biscuit-fuelled head.

Aboard the boat and parked, we could appreciate the social change, the alteration in mass scenery. The ubiquitous Thai smile had given place to diffident, sad looking Indians and stern-eyed, unforthcoming Chinese. In between were beauteous lady flowers, draped in *chador* shawls, tunics and ankle length skirts. Next to the 'Girls Who Must Eat' and the occidental women in their nipply, peekaboo tank tops, there was such local decorum, such elegant modesty, that although, by their standards, I was decently dressed (in a cotton shirt and pants), I felt not quite a woman: I was missing an essential 30 per cent of wisdom and demureness, not to mention the saris. The Indian women managed to look sedate and chaste, even with five inches of midriff flashing between shimmers of firmly bound nylon. Next to them, I was androgynous at best, an Anthony Perkins or Patti Smith type of person.

We waited, dripping on the benches, for the ferry to disgorge its crowd and when the last passenger was already on the pier, we slowly walked down the gangplank, inch by painful inch, and onto the shores of Penang.

'With its quaint buildings and sleepy anachronisms, who could *not* love Georgetown?' gushed the guidebook.

I had expected to see porticoes and horse-drawn carriages and mango juleps – some kind of pre-bellum

Savannah but, on first inspection, it was more like the Gowanus Canal: iron scraps, cranes, rubbish, dead fish and a background of warehouses that formed an ungainly daisy chain of cement blocks.

A species of armoured taxi waited self-importantly next to the unloading ramp, but when Pierre tried to engage one, the driver scoffed at him.

'White Horse Hotel too close! Only mile! I go too far!' We had to settle for two Malaysian bicycle taxis, where we sat, this time in front, while the driver pushed from the back. We flew forth – advancing mastheads – into the quiet streets, newly arrived and on review. As the clock struck one o'clock on the cantilevered veranda, we skidded and squeaked into the dusty driveway of the White Horse, 'a decent, clean, five dollar a night Chinese hotel.'

Now, this part was right out of the classic Western, when the preacher's little family gets off the stagecoach, clutching all their belongings, only to stand smack in the middle of the chuckling hyenas who've taken over the town. As we neared the porch, a party of easy riders, wearing T-shirts like 'ENJOY GOLDEN TRIANGLE' and sporting lots of matted hair, shifted their beers and butts to get a better look. Of course we *were* odd: Pierre, pale as cornstarch, dressed in black linen and holding his paper bag of medicine; Ava, with her Lolita heart-shaped sunglasses, peeking out from under the crocodile visor, and me, a bulky pony express, weaving like a Chinese junk and, unbeknown to me at that moment, streaked from forehead to chin with chocolate. But they didn't have to squint at us like that, or blow smoke rings as we passed, or hee-haw as if we were some kind of missionary geeks invading their drug reserve.

The Chinese prison warden at the Formica desk narrowed his eyes to a thin line and looked us over carefully before conceding a bathroom. The signs above his head said: 'NO SMOKING IN ROOMS. DOORS LOCKED AT MIDNIGHT. NO CREDIT CARDS ACCEPTED. CHECK-OUT TIME 9A.M. NO FOOD IN ROOMS. NO OVERHEAD FANS AFTER MIDNIGHT. NO UNREGISTERED PERSONS IN ROOMS.' Coming coddled and loved from the Silom, I smarted under all these interdictions: what were we then? Parolees? Rascals?

The room itself was really dog-eared: gangrene green, bars on the windows, melted linoleum on the floor, *no sheets*. The most depressing factor was the big pair of espadrilles sitting complacently next to the door – somebody's enormous shoes invading our room – a couple of smelly intruders. I watched Pierre, rubbing his hands in recognition of the good old days. *Now we're living, huh? You're absolutely sure that this is the real 'us'?* I bitched with my muscles and sphincter, without words.

We dropped our bags and clothes and showered with our eyes open, trying to get as much moisture as possible back into our dehydrated bodies.

The streets of Penang at two in the afternoon were fuzzy with heat, humidity and unidentifiable disease spores. Arcades fronted the shops, but they were so narrow that we had to walk single file, either in the deep gutter, or on the sizzling street. A nice, moderate amount of runaway rubbish lent the necessary backdrop to this rough new theatre.

The only restaurant we could bear to find was a noodle room that looked like a barber shop and smelt of roasting pork. The service, which was friendly, was also so rapid that 20 minutes later we were out on the pavement again. It was now half past two, but we had no plans for the afternoon – do onions and carrots make plans inside a pressure cooker? We couldn't breathe. It was so hot we could only grope our way back to our room.

Pierre slept, abandoning me to a long afternoon of Go Fish, Pick-Up-Sticks, Hangman, and Checkers. After an hour of august boredom, I forced Ava to do some Greek declensions. The nominative went down easily but I became tongue-tied by the genitive. *She's not old enough for the genitive*, I lamented. *It's the recreative, the relative that she craves. What can be the destiny of this uprooted, Franco-American child, sitting on a sheetless bed in a Chinese hotel, reciting Greek nouns and sipping sterilised water? President of the World Health Organisation? International call girl? Globe trotting agent for Disney Products?* Whilst I was fretting, she fell asleep. I could finally relax for the first time in 29 hours.

Caught in the middle of two snoring organisms, I went outside for a drink. The aggressive afternoon had banished most of the guests to their armoured rooms. There was only a solitary blond man, decked out in roomy shorts and hiking boots sitting at the bar, smoking. I asked the manager for a Coke and waited while he rinsed a plastic cup. Stuck over the counter on the walls and doors were traveller's messages:

Patty Roschak: Flying to KL tonight. It's now or never. Sorry about you-know-what. Have a good life. Jason

Will the person who 'borrowed' my book, *Mystical Asia*, please have a good read and the decency to leave it at the desk?

Burnt out? Sick of the hassle? We are a small Islamic community of disillusioned world citizens who have found harmony and order with the tribes of the Cameroon Highlands. If you are interested AND sincere call Fatima McGreen – Tanah – 46-25-18

FOR SALE:
1 good pair of heavy cotton socks
2 paperbacks – *Hold Your Head Up And Die*
         The Portrait of Dorian Gray
1 metallic green Ronson lighter
Ask manager for info

Female Travelling Companion Wanted – 20–30 yrs, free spirit, no hang-ups, driver's license. Germans need not reply – Michael Lipman Room 21

'Have you been travelling for a long time?'

I was so busy writing that it took me a few moments to realise that the question had been directed at me. I looked up at the blond man, who had stopped writing to dip his droopy moustache into a glass of beer. The empty porch was stone silent and full of the unanswered question still quivering in the overhead chimes.

'Unh . . .' It was the kind of query that asked for a pocket biography.

'Just a few weeks,' I said.

'You look like you've had a lot of experience? There is nothing confused about your face? If you understand what I mean?'

'Unh . . .'

'My name is Clemens? I'm from Salzburg? I'm travelling for quite some time, so I see many confused people? I am one of them? But it's nice to find a person who is sure of things?'

I couldn't figure out if all Austrians spoke with a lilting accent or if he were lacking confidence in a foreign language.

'*I'm* not confused?' I laughed. 'I barely know what country I'm in. My husband gets furious because I keep calling this place "Indonesia".'

His eyes, green, like the kryptonite that used to weaken Superman, radiated light from some passive humour that was hidden deep inside his nineteenth-century head.

'This is not confusion – it is only disorganisation? Maybe you don't like to have factual responsibility? There is a practical plane and a metaphysical plane that don't necessarily go together?'

Hey, man, I thought, *you don't just meet a person and zap her with philosophical fast food. This kind of talk is for after midnight in a tiny Romanian restaurant, at the end of the chocolate mousse and before the cognac. How can you throw out suffixes like -ity, -ical and -ion, when the air is hotter than body temperature and the only way to get a deep breath is by carefully yawning?*

He had an attractive bone structure, the blasé safari man in cigarette commercials, and he seemed to think of me as a kind of adventurous Jane Fonda. I could stand it.

'Are you on holiday?' I asked, avoiding the convoluted theories that held him in thrall and trying for some easy listening predicates.

He stared at me with the concentration of a snake shedding its skin.

'You could say I'm on a long journey?' he answered. 'I was a computer programmer for seven years when, one day I said, "This is enough? Seven years is enough with machines? I will stop now?"'

'Good for you!' I approved. 'So, you simply took off for Asia, from one day to the next?'

This was fabulous news: computer programmers were free falling through the universe again. There was still hope for those millions of human appliances, tragically plugged into machines and forced to carry the burdens of the next two centuries on their crouching backs.

'Not exactly?' he corrected me. 'The real idea came when I went with some friends to a hydroelectric dam in Anghoven, one weekend, to see the operating unit and to talk with the engineers? Well, there was a problem because something was blocking one of the filters, so we had to go and clean it out? We were pulling rocks and leaves, but something else, very large, was sticking through. When we finally took it out, after pulling like crazy for a long time, it was something like a dark, nasty branch, but so big . . . too big to be a branch? It had a head about the size of a small motor – with two distinct eyes and something like a face? It was twilight by the time we brought it up, this 'thing', but I became very dizzy – I was rushing through the cosmos? I heard screaming and sadness, and I fainted and fell in the water of the dam?'

'Wow!'

'I never had so much fear? I can say this was a terrible experience? After they pulled me out of the water, they got the 'thing' out completely and they threw it over the other side. Then we all went back to the station for me to get dried and to have some coffee? We sat there, my friends and I, just looking like this?'

He tilted his head forward, his mouth hung open and showed an emptiness around the eyes.

'Both of my friends experienced the same thing; they said it had been like rushing through an endless room with no air. We could barely drink our coffee, only stare and stare at the wall? I didn't go back to work on Monday, but I went to buy a plane ticket and gave my apartment to a friend. A few days later I was in Bangkok?'

I had certainly been right about him free falling through the universe!

'What do you think you're looking for, then?' I wanted to know. 'I mean in this particular part of the world?'

'The shape.'

He wasn't smiling now; there was a petulant tightness around his nose that indicated a very slight derangement. He took out a folded road map of Southeast Asia.

'If you look here, if you see this peninsula, take away Burma, yes there, but you keep to the long thin outline of southern Thailand and continue down, like this, very narrow and then through Malaysia, it is identical? Yes, *identical* with the proportions of the 'thing' that we found. Singapore is there at the bottom like the mouth. It is like a photocopy of our discovery?'

'Is that where you're heading – to Singapore?'

'Yes. Something is waiting. You see?' *Oh my God.*

While he was gazing, transfixed, at his glass, I examined his aura and came to the conclusion that he was probably not a mythomaniac. Although he was only about thirty, he had an impressive collection of truth lines along his forehead and under his chin, wrinkles formed by years of candidly blurting out honest replies. The two receding bays of his widow's peak were most likely the result of the way he smoothed back his hair every few minutes in exasperation, in amazement at life. I had nothing to say to him after his last question mark. The five o'clock heat around my brain had short-circuited any critical powers I might have still possessed and his sing-song narration acted as a soporific, lulling me into a hound-dog stupor.

'I'm going to the bookshop,' I decided. 'It's been very interesting talking to you. I hope that whatever is waiting for you in Singapore is benign.'

'Yah?' He shrugged, 'It is what it is and I am what I am?' For my money that conversation ended just at the right moment.

The sweet Indian bookseller was trying to get rid of a 14-month-old *Geo*: 'It has an extremely important article about the Philippines, ma'am. Were you aware that President Marcos had his head carved into a mountain? There are very extraordinary pictures that you must buy – only three dollars, because you *must* have this information. I will lose but you will gain ma'am.'

I hesitated, looking for something more substantial. The shelves were lined with American and English paperbacks, exhausted by their odysseys, spines broken and spotted with curry stains and rain. The choice was surprising: Burgess, Azimov, Gogol, George Sand, Thomas Hardy, Camus, Cervantes, Borges, Gertrude Stein. Relieved after the Stephen Kings and the *How to Meditate Your Way to Millions* of the airports and hotel lobbies, I chose Henry Miller, my old buddy once again – that blade.

Chapter Ten

Forsan Et Haec Olim Meminisse Iubavit
(Perhaps some day even these things will be pleasant to remember)

The evening reopened the bazaars, their jars and buckets of wriggling merchandise filling the stores and pavements and overflowing onto the more dignified territories of the silk merchants who kept up endless tirades against the invasion. Walking along the road we could have purchased an artificial hand, a ten ounce bag of red spiders, rose petal paste, rooster urine, ivory teeth, and six packs of extracted snake venom.

We were dying for a healthy, vegetable curry that would have a little something for all three of us, that we could eat with a smile. We chose a noisy Indian diner called 'The Excellent Restaurant', and slid into a wooden booth.

The table was carved with graffiti several millimetres deep, earthy reminders of 'Harold', 'Amanda', 'Jean-Luc', 'Klaus', 'Eric', 'Bettina' and bordered with miniature obscenities and Nazi insignia. Wherever you skittered to on this unwholesome planet, you could always be sure that mediocrity had already arrived and was lounging in a nearby hammock, scratching its crotch.

A pleasant waiter came over and offered the menu, which announced:

Some curries
One mutton curry

One chicken curry
One vegetable curry
One fish curry some paratas
Some chapatis

When the food arrived, Ava's 'plain' chapati was stuffed with very hot, spicy yoghurt and onions, but when I tried to clean it out, Pierre got angry.

'Can't you leave her alone? Does she have to be pampered like Pu Yi, the last emperor of China?'

'But she can't eat diabolo sauce,' I argued, 'this is not an adult. This is one child.'

'And you are one typical mother hen. Look.'

He *would* demonstrate.

'Ava, you want to eat this stuffed chapati, don't you? You like yoghurt, right? You don't mind a little chilli sauce, do you?'

Ava sat with her chin in her neck, thinking. She lifted the rubbery edge of her pancake, broke off a piece and nibbled.

'There, you see!' he exclaimed. 'You just take care of your vegetable curry and let the rest of the world breathe.'

'You unfeeling frog!' I counterattacked, raising my voice and my fork. (Food was always a problem between us; Pierre, being French, was very emotional about the art of cookery and the suitability of certain ingredients, but at the same time determined that Ava should stoically accept anything that was put on her plate).

'She hasn't had a proper meal in three days and you want to scald her palate! All you can think of is your own precious heart. What's good for you is good for her. I'm sick of it.'

As I shifted my head in punctuation, I glanced into the faces of four Hindus standing by, alert to every nuance of our fight. Behind them other Indian clientele were halfway out of their seats, eagerly waiting for more.

'Let's just shut up,' I suggested.

We ate angrily, unhealthily, while Ava harvested what she could.

That night we lay fitfully, drenched and scabby against notched mattresses. I dreamed that I was supposed to take an important Latin test, my entire future at stake. When I tried to enter the classroom, Imelda Marcos, dressed up in a nun's wimple, barred my way, saying that she was sorry but I was too unkempt to be admitted. I begged her to let me in, 'I know the *Aeneid* by heart. I can quote all of Virgil,' but she ranted over and over in a shrill, nasal voice, 'We can't take the chance, you might be infected, we can't take the chance, you might be infected . . .'

We awoke, rested and subdued, to the solo drone of the muezzin that prised us out of bed and encouraged us into the shower.

For breakfast we went to a nearby café that screamed through its windows: 'Cornflaiks, Bacon-egg, Toest, Pancakes, Mashbrows'.

A young girl in a greasy T-shirt took our orders, then proceeded to crouch over a hole in the floor to kindle a fire for our coffee. A grey coathanger of a cat lay in the middle of a pile of discarded Pepsi tops nursing three, scraggy, bleating kittens. The cat seemed to be winking at me in the sketchy half-light, but as I focused on its head, the features became distinct and I saw that several cockroaches were crawling around on top of its eyes and in and out of its ears. I did some of those natural childbirth breathing exercises, and forced myself to under-react. We *needed* this food to be able to walk. This was Asia, remember? Not Cedar Rapids, Iowa. We had bought round trip tickets for this, cockroaches included.

One by one, the tables filled up with occidental youths dressed in drawstring karate pants, lederhosen, pedal pushers and groin enhancers. It was a school textbook illustration of 'The People of the World', all in native costume, but clamouring in one voice for that satisfying American roadhouse fare.

I screamed and jerked my cup in the air, splashing coffee over already sticky heads. I just couldn't help it; when I see a cockroach suddenly like that, scooting across my own table, my reflexes reverse and I lose total physical control.

'Maman!' protested Ava.

Pierre clutched his heart and took a napkin to wipe his streaming face. The boys right next to him jumped up and shook droplets off their biceps. Everybody else in the place reprimanded me severely with their foreheads. Twenty-five-year-old sensitivities had been offended, cool had been misplaced and several nationalities had been sprayed. As the Beatles would have put it, I was a 'stupid get'.

After breakfast, we decided to do something really abysmal: go looking for the 'ravishing little hotel, set on a fairytale lagoon,' that the guidebook assured us was a few miles from Georgetown. We took a bicycle to the bus station, where we then waited half an hour for a public vehicle to come our way. For our patience, we got sucked into an airless huddle of pious women who stood and crouched with pristine unconcern, while Pierre and I sweated like cotton pickers.

The driver never left first gear as he swerved from grocery store to goat shed to the turn-off for the Silk Hanky Discotheque to post box to fruit stand. It was all very folkloric and would have even been entertaining *with* oxygen. The driver, who held a running conversation with a *chador* – that's all I could see, a *chador* chattering – eventually stopped on a steep cliff overlooking a tiny bay and turned to us yelling, 'You must get off this bus, *now*!'

We had asked him to indicate at what point we were to disembark, but anyone listening would have thought we'd been mooning or throwing beer cans. He stood up at his seat, pointed straight into our eyes and ordered us to, 'Go down quickly!'

Following his stern directions, we descended onto the mushy tarmac and just missed being juiced by a careering beverage truck. We walked very carefully along the winding, treacherous road until we reached the spot indicated by the driver. It was indeed lovely: a white, colonial cottage with roses and porch swings, but the sign on the gatepost said 'Closed for Renovation'. A monkey screamed down at us from one of the towering palm trees. There was nothing else: no taxis, no buses, no cafés, no pavement – only highway and heat.

Once again, I could trace the blame to Pierre. Why had it been so important to save six measly Malaysian dollars, the difference between the bus and the taxi? This was the price of a small cauliflower in Paris, a dish cloth in Greece – and we had saved it! We walked tightrope along the grassy strip that bordered the road, the last human family at the end of the world.

Ava soon managed to step on an antediluvian worm the size of an eggplant, and the valley below echoed a resounding, '*Merrrrde!*'

Some hot-shot Malaysian rich kids whipped by in a custom made convertible, slowed down to catch our act, then accelerated with farty insolence. I was so thirsty by this time I could have licked the slime from Ava's shoe but retained the energy for the stockpile of grievances that I was building up against her father. That six dollars kept flashing through my mind and needling me like a detail in a Saki short story.

When I stopped and collapsed under a banana tree, Ava flung herself into my arms crying, 'I've got a stomach ache.' I looked at my watch. Sure enough, it was one o'clock, my favourite time of the day. Overzealous crickets that had not yet given up for the morning cheeched in the surrounding bushes. Dense clouds of insects conscientiously lugged their germs from one tree to another.

After 15 minutes of silence, Pierre suddenly jumped up, ran over to the road and hailed a passing taxi. I don't know how exactly he did that, whether it was the concentrated will-power of the physically impaired or if he'd simply placed one of his bionic ears against the tree trunk and heard diesel vibrations. In any case,

I lost considerable foundation for my vengeance programme and was pressured into the small talk of reconciliation. This didn't last longer than a 'Look at that strange rock formation', because the taxi went into a running speed of a 100 mph along the zigzagging road and Ava threw up all over our knees. I leaned toward the driver to tell him to slow down but, although most Malaysians speak very good English, this was beyond his understanding. He continued to rip through the countryside and Ava continued to vomit.

How much punishment could mammals take? I felt like a ewe watching her lamb being slaughtered for cutlets. Could we have slid inadvertently onto a woebegone plateau, the good life behind us forever?

From that moment until eight o'clock at night is a blank to me now. It wasn't the nadir but the limbo-esque pre-nadir, impossible to recall. I don't know if we stayed in the hotel room and sucked on the mattresses or if we bought cans of spam in the Soldier of Fortune grocery store across the alley. I only remember that the afternoon was a couple of tranquillisers long and that it was followed by a night of even heavier penance.

From under hermetically closed eyelids, I could hear the hairbrush *whoosh-whooshing* around Ava's head. I could make out the whistle of the shower, the slap of Pierre's feet on the linoleum and then the loud shuffling of his roomy khakis sliding up his legs.

I figured they had made plans, that they were heading somewhere, that I could risk waking up, no demands forthcoming. The solitary overhead neon bulb lit up random objects across the room, objects that kept surviving one fiasco after another: the blue towel with the pink flamingos, a softly kneaded map of South East Asia, the crocodile suncap, Autan mosquito repellent, the small, tinted bottle of nitroglycerine. A spider web of objects holding us together.

'We're going to the Oklahoma Yippee I-O Steak Round-up Restaurant!' declared Ava, now pushing her hair into a high pony-tail with a flowered band.

'Where?'

Pierre sat down on the bed and put my legs on his lap.

'I saw it down the block when we went out last night. It's some kind of restaurant club that has big quilted doors like a speakeasy. I think it's because they're selling illegal vegetables. I saw corn and squash advertised – and fresh salad. Go and get dressed.'

'I can't,' I said. 'I couldn't bear another series of calamities. You go by yourselves. It must be me that's the albatross. Besides, I need to read – to escape. Hey, you know this story? Henry Miller is working in this nine to five job in New York and he has all these friends and it's so ordinary that . . .'

'I know the book,' he said, looking at me strangely.

'Order two T-bones for Ava and bring me three of anything and a cold beer.'

When they left I remained on my left side, too relieved to move. How spoilt, to have all the space of a room to oneself. How quiet and empty it was, and how unmovable my book looked on the floor. My eyes shifted to the intruding espadrilles that were still parked next to the door. Every time I saw them a terrible fury ripped through my arteries and I could feel violence glowing like coal in the lower regions of my torso; they represented to me 'The Uncalled For', 'The Smelly Unknown'. I reached for my nail scissors and crawled across the room to put an end to their particular effrontery: first, fringes, then little strips along the sides, big holes for the toes, then the heels and bumps around the seams. It was perfect sitting there in my underwear, pretending I was Catherine Deneuve in *Repulsion*.

When I had finished and thrown the whole mess into the wastepaper basket, I walked into the shower and turned on the water. There was a sickening tear – not unlike the sound of scissors on cloth – a crash, and a punishment of rain that sounded more like a giraffe stampede than a cloudburst. At home by now, in this universe of hourly drama, I continued to soap and rinse, in spite of the fearful clatter of a thousand typewriters writing some divine headline. I smiled idiotically; it was a funny coincidence, cutting up the shoe, then right away, thunder.

Before I could go on with this nonsense, the outside door of the room banged open and the Chinese owner ran in screaming, 'Off lights! Off shawa! Off! Off!'

He flicked the wall switch. I stopped my tap before grabbing a sarong in case of other invasions. Now it was totally dark and hysterically noisy. I was witnessing my first real Declaration of Water. It was also perplexing: an atmospheric jam session that I had never experienced before. Would the roof hold up? The windows break? I dried off and felt around for my T-shirt and shorts. Then a third noise vied for ear space, a horizontal gushing on two sides of the hotel, the noise of sewers in their hey-day, feverish currents running to their rendezvous.

When I looked out of the window I could see more than a foot of hurrying black outlined against the cement wall. The droning continued, oblivious to the harmony of nature; it was neurotic, obsessed with getting there. I stuck my head out the door, and far down the hall I saw streaming blond heads, soggy moustaches and hands sloughing off water. Then Pierre appeared with all 35 kilos of Ava in his arms, lurching towards me. I ran to meet them.

'No more than *five* kilos! Put her down! You'll kill yourself!'

'I lost my shoes, Mummy.'

'We got stuck in the gutter. It was two feet deep!'

'We couldn't go to the Oklahoma Yippee I-O Steak Round-up Restaurant. The water was up to my pockets.'

'I had to carry her for three blocks. It was crazy the things we saw floating: bottles, wooden planks, apples, batteries . . .'

They were densely wet as if covered with Vaseline, making it difficult to peel off the stiff outfits.

'So you didn't eat?'

'Of course not. Did they eat during the San Francisco earthquake? Besides, we've only been gone for fifteen minutes.'

'I'm so hungry, Mummy!'

She was sitting on the bed in her underpants, her chest caved in, red patches on her cheeks. Pierre lay flat out, pale, gasping for air.

'Isn't there anything to eat here in the hotel?' I ventured.

'Potato chips,' whispered Pierre.

'Well, we just have to wait it out, then.'

'I see white ghosts in front of my eyes, Mummy.'

'I'm going.'

I slipped on my rubber sandals, grabbed a wad of Malaysian dollars and left.

On the threshold of the hotel the other guests were having a rain party. Clustered beneath the cement porticos they sang national anthems and floundered in the knee-deep mud. By the looks of it, I would have to wait. It was impossible to think of taking to the streets: I'd be washed away.

I sat beside the cold-drink fridge, looking out at the squat buildings and iron grill work that barred most of the windows. This was a commercial centre, built for products and their warehouses, not for people. There were no parks or yards, only shops and hastily built dwellings of some inauspicious period. No hygienic second thoughts: litter strewn wherever, gangs of roaming dogs and cats – peevish, calculating strays. While the Malaysians and Indians seemed to have made some compromise between work and cleanliness, the Chinese were like seller robots, uninterested in any activity that excluded profit.

There was such tightness in their regard, such steady concentration on *transaction,* and besides that – chaos: squashed tomatoes gathering fungus underneath sun lotion displays, broken glass swept forever into a corner, stepping stones of animal corpses in varying stages of decay, labyrinthine trails of spit.

The radio crackled and some far away disc-jockey in Singapore dug deep in his collection of pirate cassettes to produce Johnny Mathis singing 'Misty'. A wonderful 30-year-old type of man-boy, whom I'd noticed reading on the terrace several times, was perched on the ramp in swimming trunks wading in the puddles.

When the song started he impulsively turned to the girl next to him, a pretty curly-haired French tourist and pulled her into the yard to dance. The rain soaked them within seconds, but the moment was vital and they were oblivious to the weather. Her silver T-shirt disappeared as the water made it one with her skin and her shorts shrivelled up against her derrière. The boy's muscles were magnified by the shadings of night and rain, his arms firm and veined around her slender back. They danced politely at first, then closer and closer until they were swaying and quietly inhaling. This was genuine 'love at first sight' personally observed, as visually rare as a four-leaf clover or perfect teeth.

The shower was over before the song, so I went forward on my food-gathering mission. I had to walk in the streets, or rather, on the mounds in the middle that curved down into trenches against the tiny useless footpaths. These trenches were now on duty, protecting the stores or stockrooms, passing whirlpools from one street to another. Skimming the water was an affluence of soda cans, shoes, newspapers and even a stray bra.

When I arrived at the crossroads, the high ground had disappeared, leaving only a smooth body of water that lapped at the tops of the parked car wheels. I doubled back to the street before the hotel which turned out to be practically dry and where tables and soup pots were being dragged out for the evening business. I walked until I came to the Indian shop of the previous night, where they knew me, indeed, where they knew *exactly* what was on my mind, and stopped at the window opening in front of the grill.

'Hello,' said one of the dozen personnel, 'what can I make for you?'

I was wet and sticky and my feet were making indecent noises inside my rubber shoes. I, nevertheless, tried to focus on the restrictions imposed by youth and clogged arteries: no meat, no butter – no grease of any kind – no eggs, no sauces, no cakes for Pierre. No spices, no fish, no tomato sauce, no onions, no garlic for Ava.

'Six paratas, please, and three plain yoghurts and a half chicken, but no butter, no fried.'

'No butter, Miss,' he agreed, throwing six pancakes on the grill and before I could blink, dousing them in oil.

'*No* oil!' I cried desperately, 'No *grease*! I'm sorry, but my husband is sick, you see. He can't have oil: no fried. *Just* grilled.'

Surprised, then worried, he gathered up the paratas, wiped them with a handful of paper napkins and threw them back on the grill. He was very accommodating. I stared over the cook's head into the store, watching the other waiters watching me. I felt a scurrying and a tickling on my foot – probably another trickle of flood water or a flying sweet wrapper.

As I glanced down, I came face to face with a rodent the size of a small dog – well it was at least 6 or 12 inches, depending on whether or not you like to include the tail. The horrible bubonic creep had nonchalantly *walked*, not run, over my exposed feet. When I nearly fainted against the glass counter, the cook was very pleased; he flashed fluorescent teeth and said softly, 'You have a very interesting nose, Miss.'

Then, completely disconcerted by my facial structure, he dipped a soup ladle into a bucket of clarified butter and sprinkled it mechanically over my order.

Meanwhile, the rat was still lurking. It had strolled into the corner of the doorway and crouched there, nibbling on a bone that could just as easily have been one of my toes. The waiters stood a few feet from it, smoking cigarettes and watching the passing tourists. From time to time, they eyed the rat but did nothing to chase it away. The thing was definitely cognito, a comfortable symbol of the town's prospering netherlife.

I paid the man and gathered up the big, spotted bag that bulged in all directions and dripped down the front of my shirt. I walked back to the hotel cursing the guidebooks and the rat, that typhoid-bearing little criminal.

Back in the room, Ava was languid, gazing at the overhead fan. Pierre had a fever. I took the paratas out and spread them on the bed, on top of napkins and newspaper. There was a feeble stirring at the rustling of the bag, but neither of them had the life force to chew. Ava took a few desultory bites and fell back on the pillow. Pierre wet his lips with the yoghurt.

'Friends,' I said, 'we've had it. You see this brochure that Ava picked up at the bus station? You see this Kon Tiki Hotel at Ferringhi Beach? The one with the

Hollywood driveway and the swimming pool in the shape of a dolphin and the waterslide? The one with the jungle bar and the sauna and the *six* different restaurants and the Bora Bora Lounge? We're moving in! Tomorrow! Right after breakfast in the Cockroach and Coffee Shop next door.'

They barely heard me, so great was their apathy. Pierre didn't have the slightest financial objection and Ava didn't whisper '*La vie est belle!*'

I hoped it wouldn't be too late.

Chapter Eleven

I Think My Mother Would Like One of These Coathangers

'Good morning to you!' cried an impeccably groomed young woman in a shantung dress and choker pearls. 'I'm this year's Miss Kon Tiki. I would like to welcome you to our hotel.'

From the pastel wicker basket by her side, she drew out three orchids, 'With the compliments of our staff.'

She radiated like a lighthouse ushering in small craft.

We accepted this homage that gave us the right to a debonair porter with 'KTs' entwined around his shirt. He led us to the elevator, pushed the 'up' button and tried to snare us into a decent, well-rehearsed conversation.

'Is this your baby?' he asked, stroking Ava's head. 'She looks like Brooke Shields. Very nice. You like Brooke Shields, baby?'

The elevator had glossy advertising for 'South Pacific Night every Wednesday – Lobsters, Polynesian Cocktails, Barbecue and Appearing This Week: The Coconut Melody Makers, with the chanteuse, Charlotte Lee, Happy Chip on the guitar, and Buzzy Ho at the piano.'

There was another picture on the opposite wall of a Saturday night rock and roll blast featuring Carla and the Petticoats, a neo-Supremes group of heavily made-up Malaysian foxes in beehive hair-dos and party dresses with spaghetti straps. We arrived at a sixth floor doused in coral dream light, a hallway made in heaven and a blushing antechamber to *the* room.

It was another luxury zone: one square acre of plush nylon carpeting, the kind you walk barefoot through and your toes come out all clean, two king-sized beds and one princeling, a know-it-all bar crammed with celery extract, four kinds of bourbon, Perrier and Veuve Clicquot. On the frilly vanity table stood a 21-inch menu with such room service snacks as 'Imperial Capon Club Sandwich garnished with radish twists and pickled eggs. Smoked Quiche Rolls. Chicken pot Pielettes in White Wine Gravy and Roasted Croutons with Salmon and Dill Dip.' *Sacré bleu!*

On the desk were the Kon Tiki dry cleaning tariffs, Kon Tiki stationery, Kon Tiki complimentary combs and after-shave, and most intriguing, a Kon Tiki list of room furnishings that you could buy and take home as souvenirs:

Kon Tiki Wastepaper basket – 15 MD
Kon Tiki Coathanger – 2 MD
Kon Tiki Rubber Bath Mats – 6MD

The wall-to-wall, floor-to-ceiling bay window gave us a cinemascopic view of the jungle. Once in a while a monkey would catapult by and Ava would yell, 'A monkey!'

When she tired of the spectacle, she poked the remote control switch near her bed. On the very first attempt she came up with a Daffy Duck cartoon jamboree galloping across the giant TV screen in a frenzy of primary colours. This gave Pierre and me the chance to have a reasonable conversation; something we'd sorely lost the hang of.

'You have to admit . . . ' I said.

'Yes. No. OK,' admitted Pierre. 'There is something to be said for extreme comfort. I don't actually *mind* this vodka I'm sipping or the prospect of *too* much crab, or the pool with the floating trays, but there is a price to pay and you know it.'

'I know zero. For me there is nothing but relief. At this point the only thing I care about is not caring.'

'*D'accord*, let's just consider these *principalities*, these *reserves*, as hospitals – clean, therapeutic, hushed sanatoriums. That's how we have to look at it. But . . .'

He stopped speaking and frowned at Daffy, pummelled into an accordion by a wolf in lumberjack's clothing.

'. . . it wasn't what I had in mind when we decided to come to Asia. It's such a joke.'

'But heart attacks weren't on the agenda either, or staying in one place for weeks on end. You have to be taken care of properly, and Ava has to be amused and fed, and I need . . .'

'What?'

'Boredom. A sweet, silent variety of stagnation. The kind where you start counting the stripes on the bedspread, where you try to remember all the girls you've ever known whose first name began with C. That's what I need.'

'Why don't we go home, then?' he grumbled. 'What's the point in paying sixty dollars a night for embossed monotony?'

'First of all, you know that although Greece may be a lot of things, it's far from boring; all that passion and misunderstanding and Turkish coffee is exhausting. Second of all, we have to wait a little while longer, until the weather and you are fit. If we go back today, tomorrow we'll have to lug gas bottles and push the car when it stalls. I'm not ready yet. I want to stay here for a while, where fantasy and folly are moot.'

'What does "moot" mean?'

'It means maybe yes, maybe no. Something like . . . We're probably crazy but so what?'

Later in the mint green, trellised lunchroom we were attacked by a Chinese waiter dressed like Pat Boone who propelled us with his body and Magna Carta-sized menus towards a preordained wicker table.

'Trinks! Trinks!' he demanded.

'Not yet,' I tried to speak firmly, 'we'll decide what we want to eat first.'

'Fust, trinks!' he repeated undeterred, then getting no satisfaction from us, he turned roughly to Ava and barked, 'Baby, trink Coca-Cola? One Coca-Cola, yes?'

'Leave us alone, goddamit!'

Pierre raised his voice for the first time since 19 January and the waiter deflated faster than a Greek drachma. His whole personality changed and he adopted the mien of a barefoot peasant – even his fancy clothes looked too big for him. He hastily departed through a plastic, rose-covered door. We barely had time to breathe a couple of 'aie-aie-aie's when a little Bo Peep materialised, in ruffles and laced bodice, to take our orders. Same scenario, same results, except that she stood her ground, like a rejected housewife claiming more alimony. But we stood our ground, we had to. The menu contained about 85 chef's specialities, plus the Malaysian dishes, plus humorous anecdotes to wade through. In spite of her tongue-clicking and glances at the clock, we managed to scan the menu and roughly translate the ornate descriptions.

'I'll have the "Businessmen's low-cal broiled fish,"' said Pierre, at last, as if the thought had suddenly occurred to him.

'And I'll have the "Southern Fried Bayou Shrimp with Dumplings".'

'Me,' said Ava, 'I want the "Owl and the Pussycat Peanut Butter and Jelly Sailboats".'

'Isn't this pleasant!' Pierre said to nobody in particular.

I'm lying on my back, staring up at little green and red watermelons that decorate my hot pink chaise-lounge canopy. Pierre is playing ping-pong with a young Chinese merchant. Ava is splashing in the pool with some little Irish girls. A few feet away from me, a local boy, in loincloth for the occasion, is shimmying up a 40-foot palm tree in order to hack off coconuts with a machete for the awed ladies below. He throws them down rather recklessly; one could easily fall on my head. The loudspeakers are transmitting 'Moon River', the absolute number one favourite of my high-school graduating class; it was the theme tune to the film Breakfast at Tiffany's.

All the girls I went to school with imagined – assumed – they would end up like this: poolside, horizontal, devoured by leisure. This had been a national goal, to walk barefoot on expensive tiles and flash tasteful bikinis. I could never stand that Jackie Kennedy vision of 'culture', that lack of ambition. Yet, here I am, like a two-faced evangelist, catching a little action while I can.

'Come here, ya little hoppin' moondrop, little pancake face, and tell yer old Dad ya love 'im.'

A merry alto sang out charming blarney from somewhere behind me.

'What'd ya' do wit' yer schemin' sister then old Helen head, old pork chop? Where is she? Tell daddy bear before he licks off all the honey from yer face.'

Growls and shrieks vibrated along the tiles.

'Juicy eyes, little oyster snacks for the Daddy's wet tongue.'

I turned around and pushed up my sunglasses to get a look at this uprooted leprechaun. It was rare to come across a travelling Irishman, complete with brogue and poetry. He was about 36, with black hair and black eyes, squarish build, reclining like myself and holding a Vintage paperback, which seemed to be *De Profondis* by Oscar Wilde – a reader! A man of words! My God! My heart thumped like a dog's tail when he hears the sound of a can opener. My breathing got close to the surface, centred around my chin. I felt a painful yearning for elliptical syntax and grammatical minutiae and the tenderness of baby suckling metaphor.

'Well! Here she comes, the Marilyn question and her little toe buds flappin'. Come tell yer Dad what the water said and I'll tell ya if it's lyin'.'

This was divine! How could I get into a conversation with this magician? I instinctively turned toward the ping-pong table as if troubled by some oblique infidelity to Pierre. I saw that he and his partner had abandoned their game for the bar. No one was around, neither the 'towel man' nor the 'bat and ball' man. The corner was deserted. I sauntered to the edge of the pool and called, 'Ava! Do you want to play ping-pong?'

'Yay! Youpie!' she yelled. 'Wait. I'm coming!'

Poor manipulated infant. I put on my Chinese shirt, gathered up my possessions and walked towards the Irishman.

'Excuse me, but do you know if we can just go over and take the ping-pong bats if no one's there?' I tried to sound perplexed. 'Nobody's at the desk, so I don't know who to ask.' He looked up at me.

'Take what ya want, girl,' he winked, 'yer a payin' customer I assume and we're entitled to all the sins in hell, if we want 'em.'

'Yes,' I said, 'but the bats are in the drawer behind the desk. Wouldn't that be like breaking and entering?'

'Holy Mother of Jasus!' he swore. 'You want me to get up off of my chair and show ya how it's done?'

As he laughed, I could see him examining the cover of my Henry Miller book, which I had tucked obtrusively in the crook of my arm. At that moment, Ava dripped up and pulled the towel out of my hands, causing all the other sundries to fall as offerings onto the man below. I was a little embarrassed by destiny's helping hand. He sat up, extracting my bottle of suntan lotion from between his thighs and then picked up the crocodile hat and the Greek dictionary.

'What 'er ya translatin' Henry Miller inta Greek? Now I've seen everything!'

I was delighted, having reaped much more than expected. But, before I could get into interesting explanations and witty biographical data, Ava *had* to pull on my shirt and interrupt.

'*Le ping-pong, Maman*! I'm ready!'

'There's nobody at the desk,' I argued. 'Guess we can't play now.'

I tried my best to stall, but the two attendants came charging back and I was obliged to do something I didn't want to do with all my heart: play ping-goddam-pong. I wanted to stay and fool around with the Irishman. It wasn't a flirtation, only a blithe exchange of words with a stranger.

That evening we walked along the road parallel to the sea. Once we left the strip of hotels and restaurants behind us, the beach retracted and the jungle took back some of its own, pushing vegetation across the main path and latching onto rocks and driftwood. All around us were *caw-cawings* and *twir-twirings* and *cop-copings*; everything we passed seemed to either rustle or moan.

The dirt trails leading off the road beckoned us into a dense forest that Pierre wanted to investigate. I refused categorically, arguing that, for us, it wasn't recommended; we were too prone to exaggerated story lines, too receptive to misadventure. If we had taken even ten steps into that jungle, that snarling flora, there was absolutely no chance that we would have come out unscathed, whistling show tunes.

We admired the half moon, suspended in the violet twilight. Ava remarked that it was the same colours as in her last dream, the one where she had to get a job repairing television sets for animals.

'Animals? That's funny,' said Pierre.

'No, it isn't,' replied Ava. 'All the people, all the time, are animals in my dreams.'

'You mean you never dream about human beings?'

'Never, never, except you and Daddy. You're real pink people.'

I let out my breath. At least we weren't some frightening allegorical ogres. We had, after all, human roles in her subconscious. Maybe we were doing something right.

About a mile from the hotel, we turned a ferny bend and, without any warning, came face to face with *Tales From The Crypt*. Looming up 15 storeys over all this savage vegetation, over spontaneous, talkative wildlife, over our own bewildered earth, were two billion tons of cement, moulded and hardened into an evil hotel complex. The unfinished, frameless windows gaped like eye sockets on the petrified corpses that adorn the covers of horror magazines. I put my arm over my eyes and turned in the direction of the Kon Tiki.

'Will you please stop overreacting,' entreated Pierre. 'Just this once, wouldn't it be more relaxing to have a family stroll without a Tennessee Williams climax of some kind or another?'

'But it's grotesque!' I cried. 'It reminds me of my dream, that horrible nightmare I always have about that giant planet floating through the black galaxy toward that minuscule pea, and the minute they touch, I wake up screaming.'

'This isn't a heavenly body,' he said sardonically, 'and if you look carefully, there's no sign of a pea, *n'est-ce pas*?'

'But who could have created such a monstrosity? It's like the Club Med for the dead!'

'Who cares,' grumbled Pierre, 'that's how life is now. What are you, Emily Dickinson, unable to cope? For your information, this hotel is the same as the Kon Tiki, only the Kon Tiki is plastered and painted and full of grilled cheese sandwiches. I hate to ruin your perfect pitch but this thing is just a big hotel, nothing more, nothing less – and as abstract as a Boeing 747.'

'And you have no more aesthetic gumption than a Kon Tiki coathanger!'

'And you sound like Yves Saint Laurent! What do you want me to do, kick it?'

After dinner that evening we went to the Hawaiian Bar for a nightcap. The Irishman was there in the midst of his wife and daughters, the latter all wearing matching pinafores. Ava and the little girls ran away to the video machine alcove, leaving us to sip our flamboyant drinks in peace. How scrumptious it was to be an attractive adult in comfortable clothes, sitting in parakeet-covered armchairs, listening to a piped-in orchestral session of the Rolling Stones' greatest hits.

Brian from Cork introduced us to his theory of the 'Bermuda Shorts Phenomenon'.

'To my mind,' he said, in between gulps of his Waikiki Sling, 'they're the brain burst of a criminally insane mind. We all know that *wicked* rules the world, that the uglier the concept, the more it catches on. Bermuda Shorts are a negation of the human body, an encroachment on the sacred torso, a crawlin' fungus destroyin' hardy trunks.'

'Right!'
'Right!'
'Ah *bon*?'
'So I asks yer, where does one wear Bermuda shorts? In between yer navel and yer knees. This happens to be the most *interesting* part of the anatomy – but *only* when flowing – when connected to the rest of the physical sculpture. Alone, it's a joke. Alone, the groin resembles celery root or a chimney on a roof. Why would yer want to isolate yer bums, except for plain mockery? They're a nasty invention. Look at women when they're only dressed in brassieres; it doesn't make sense, now, does it?'

I looked over at Pierre who was listening with that special brand of harried attention that he reserves for all things exaggeratedly fanciful.

'I understand a little,' he ventured, 'that sometimes it's not very beautiful, but on everyday people like me, for instance, what is *wrong* with a Bermuda short? It's cool and practical. I don't see the problem.'

I had to intervene to thread the wool between the two different cultures.

'That's because you're French, Pierre,' I said, turning to explain to the others. 'In France they have the knack of adapting elegantly. They can take the abstract idea and create whispers of earthy golds and browns that will drape silkily over their ski tans. There's no interruption of the line. Also, French derrières are either nonexistent or so minute and firm that practically any packaging looks good. In America, on the other hand, Bermudas have the same function as big, lumpy wallets – they're where you keep your valuables, safe and unnoticed.'

'HaHaHaHaHaHa!' bellowed the Irishman. 'That's a good one, gal!'

He was an excellent audience, standing up to toast my *bon mot* whilst smacking his lips as if he'd just taken a big bite out of me.

Next to him, Patsy, the wife, began to wriggle her shoulders in time to the sterilised 'Get Off My Cloud', defending her territory. To my surprise, Brian worked up an answering shimmy, and they faced each other, these spouses, these soulmates, swapping proud, physical memories. With the rash candour of drunken optimists, they revealed a lot about their love life: Patsy, hovering over her partner, liked to be on top where she could excitedly tease him with her sultry underarms; Brian, though, wanted to be in control, snapping his fingers in her face when she got too insistent and flexing his strong hands and forearm muscles when she tangoed her breasts too close to his neck. I pondered folks who could read Oscar Wilde and be turned on by elevator music.

Chapter Twelve

Monkeys in the Rain

Breakfast at the Kon Tiki was a stupendous Brobdingnagian Feedarama, a prolific harvest of bacon, ham, sausages, whole pigs, multiple egg dishes, pancakes, waffles, biscuits, cereals, fish, cheese, breakfast steaks, croissants, rolls, Danish pastries, muffins, cappuccino, rolls smoked salmon and bagels, fruit cup: the only thing missing was whale blubber. For four dollars you could feed until your zips slid open, and some people who, honestly, didn't need to, were doing just that.

The terrace was swarming with serious bargain hunters and sexagenarians who were groping for rolls with the insides of their elbows, clutching pots of thick cream with one hand and jabbing at stacks of meat with the other. Each plate was heaped with enough cholesterol to block the Channel Tunnel; I couldn't see how some of the plates could make it from the counter to the tables. Then they went back for more. Thirds weren't unheard of. These people were obviously making up for years of lottery loss, sensory deprivation, for that lawsuit that cost them a fortune, for that exorbitant taxi fare in Singapore; this was the indemnity office. You had to stand in line, but you eventually got what was coming to you.

The Malay and Chinese waiters stood erect, their backs to the wall, observing this monomania with blank faces but alert eyes. Quite often, summoned by an arm flapping in distress, an undernourished waitress would sail over to a table to deal with such frustrations as 'lack of honey' or more and more and more coffee, or the most absurd, the continuous demand for sugar substitute. Now I understood why the service had been so frantic the first day. We had been too hesitant, too undecided, not really inclined. These were professional teams, used to complying with urgent, unmentionable needs and were trained to deal out immediate fulfilment, high voltage restoration. You didn't waste that talent on picky eaters.

Instead of hanging around the pool all day, we decided to take a picnic lunch to the botanical gardens and see about the monkeys. The guidebook said that they were so tame and charming they would eat out of our hands. However the island's English newspaper warned that, since they were multiplying so quickly – virtually taking over the eastern side of Penang – a paid posse should be sent out to destroy several thousand of them. I couldn't imagine anything worse than bounty hunting for monkeys: their little heads cocked and frightened by the smell of hunters, their shrill communications, and then shots, followed by opposable thumbs twitching in all directions. It would be like slaughtering high-strung trapeze artists – too agile and coordinated to be game.

We brought blue and white checked lunch boxes from the hotel kitchen, food especially designed for explorers like ourselves – little shish-kebabs, little cups of rice, hardboiled eggs, biscuits, pickles and pineapple slices. The Kon Tiki could now rest assured that for however long we were absent and in spite of the many buffets, brunches and luncheons missed, we would not go hungry into those dense gardens.

The taxi was owned by a certain Mohammed, as gracious as Scarlet O'Hara. He climbed out to open the doors for us, brushing the back seats with great concern before pushing us in. He got into the car, turned around to see how we looked back there and, satisfied, popped a Country and Western cassette into the machine.

The avenue to the park ran past masterpieces of Victoriana: splendid wooden houses that wound around themselves, curling up to the sky in a heady peak of turrets and gables. They were laid back from the main road and protected from the naked eye by the veils of weeping willows. We passed several churches; low, modest affairs, but even crouching, so as not to stand out too much in this Muslim outpost, they retained a spinsterish authority by their tight, elongated spires that still insisted towards paradise.

At the entrance of the gardens, Mohammed rushed around to let us out and although we tried to discourage him, insisted on waiting, no matter how long we would be. He warned us, at the same time, about 'pickpockets', 'too much heat', but, above all against monkeys: 'they no good.'

Peanut brokers lined the car park, shouting for custom and begging us to, 'Buy these nuts here, mister and sir! These are the good ones, please!'

The grounds were landscaped, claimed and hacked out of forests that peeked over the pruned trees like unruly relatives looking in at their rich cousins. The footpaths criss-crossed around floral exhibitions of genius: stalks that had happened upon fantastic secret formulas to produce flowers of humour; gorgeous, witty things that leaned out to mock other, lesser manifestations around them. Their names escape me but I can describe their victorious petals, several millimetres thick, curling into themselves seductively as though trying to embrace their own pistils. And those other prodigies, those strange lumpy deposits, about two feet high, whose black and pink stripes and blackish stems gave off a strong déja vu of zebra foetuses.

A few yards farther, triffid paws thrust out electric blue tentacles that sniffed at us as we walked by and then went slightly limp – I didn't blame them. As we crossed a plank bridge that linked the cracked banks of a dried-up river, we sighted our first monkeys, clustered together in a nervous parliament. They were fine grey and beige characters, somewhat dyspeptic. When Ava ran to them, peanut bag outstretched, they yelled and cupped their mouths like angry fans at Shea Stadium, but when she cracked the nuts and started to eat them herself, they became thoughtful, limiting their theatrics to nods and exaggerated eye movements.

We ambled by a package of Japanese tourists, uniformed in light orange safari outfits. Helmeted and bespectacled, they were examining the plants, branch by branch, their preference for stem over flower mysterious. Attached to their arms were checked cardboard boxes. Lunch? Were all foreigners so equipped by their hotels for adventure? Gone were the days of improvisation, an egg roll here, a local beer there. Serenity and security were paid for now and every step taken care of before hand.

Up the road and deeper into the bushes, a day of busy meandering was in full sway, the primates abundant and excited. Their behaviour was more than erratic; it was 'psycho-propelling', a word I invented on the spot to describe the reaction of rapidly evolving brains (crammed into skulls too small for the job) to rapidly deteriorating brains (splashing around in great big decorative heads). These monkeys were trying to mime people, but humans were utterly inimitable in their helmets and bikini tops, their crew-cuts and crotch ticklers. How was it possible, for example, for these smart little apes to imitate that Englishman sitting there slumped on the bench, with his Brighton bowling shirt rolled up under his arms, exposing much too much flab? They couldn't do it; instead, they rode piggyback, twirled around a lamp post and harangued. A delegation of four walked right up to us, as if to propose a party coalition, and then, changing their minds, stopped in their tracks to mutually examine anuses.

It was clear that the monkey population was not showing all its cards; it seemed to expect a certain discretion on our part or maybe an initiation ritual that we weren't aware of. We continued to wander and found ourselves in the jungle rush hour – alarming numbers conveying on all sides. Again, Ava stopped to pull out the bag of nuts, but before she could rustle it open, one little hooligan snatched it, sniffed it, threw the whole lot in the air, then and loped away. There was no commotion for this product, nobody was interested.

A few yards away we discovered why: two hairy mothers munched on papaya and pineapple, smacking down jealous children with expert clout. These were simian yuppies, plugged into the nineties and, like the rich Parisian teenagers who eschewed café for cappuccino and hamburgers for shrimp paté, they simply disdained peanuts as long as quality fruit was so easily available.

We walked until we found a plateau with large accessible boulders to picnic on. This was Pierre's idea. He insisted that we scale them by digging our toes into crevasses and hoisting each other up. I unpacked the food, laying it out on the hard surface – my role model, Grace Kelly in *Mogambo*.

When we leaned over the edge, we could see those little heads bobbing up and down, trying like crazy to see what we were doing. It didn't take long for highly identifiable odours to make safe landings in mini-cerebellums; then, the hands reached over the heads, flexing, blindly groping for the fruit. Ava was the first to succumb. She threw over two end slices of pineapple to the 'poor monkeys'; they were pounced upon and torn to pieces. The rumour of success drifted to surrounding areas, provoking friends and neighbours into galloping over to join in the merriment. I don't think it was the fruit so much, as the intrigue of our being a bit out of reach that sucked them around the base of our rock in droves and had them dancing little jigs.

We ate the kebabs and threw them the fatty parts, probably the right thing to do because that caused belly scratching contempt and the crowd dispersed, forming little groups of three or four taking counsel.

There should have been a warning. We should have realised that we weren't sizzling as usual in the two o'clock incandescence. It must have been obvious that the weather was moody, but we only understood when the air above us roared, a fast preamble to the hard examples of rain that fell like carving knives on our stunned heads. Before we could swear, we were soaked. The food drifted away in cardboard boats full of water and the rain enveloped the big stones in a two-inch thick cascading sheet which made descent completely inoperative. The monkeys took refuge under the trees and loitered, dry and collected, watching our predicament. We sat there, becoming heavier and heavier.

'You know what I consider to be the finest invention of the twentieth century?' asked Pierre, by way of striking up a conversation, 'Plastic garbage bags! You can use them for so many things: moving, storing, gardening, shopping, for raincoats, robbing banks; in fact, you might say that one needs a garbage bag at any given moment of the day. When I read in the newspaper accounts of the police finding a dismembered body tied up in a plastic garbage bag, my blood boils. Why don't they write something less slanderous like, "impermeable sacks" or "synthetic recipients"? To give you an example, take the wheel; the papers don't say, "Mr. François Moreau was run over by four rubber wheels," do they? No, they say, "He was hit by a black Citroën", right? They avoid smearing an innocent reputation. Why can't they do this for the garbage bag?'

We thus chatted until everything evaporated – the rain, the torrents, the monkeys. When it was possible, we slid down the glistening boulder and hit the ground with dull thuds. The way back to the car park was silent except for a few exalted birds and a couple of Indians who emerged practically dry from one of the annexes of the jungle. How come none of the other people had wet horns hanging down their faces? If the temperature had been one degree less than a 109, we would have certainly caught cold but, as it was, the air went immediately back to pre-broil, and I felt as if my features were sliding down my chin.

We came out of the garden with loads less jaunt than we had going in and we must have looked really ghoulish because Mohammed jumped out of the car, cried, 'Stop to wait! Stop to Wait!' and rushed to the trunk for old clothes which he threw over the furry pussycat covers of the backseat. We felt itchy and dirty sitting on crusty cotton shirts and threadbare towels.

Our life was now far beyond mere hazard. It was starting to become wondrous. Wherever we went, whatever we did, we could always count on things going wrong. Accepting this, I felt a tingling around my rib cage, a spiritual buoyancy. There was something soothing about coherent malediction – you didn't feel abandoned. There was even a crackpot kind of logic: since there was nothing we could do, our lot was chartered. We had to make the worst of things.

'I can't tell,' said Pierre that night, as he was getting ready for bed, 'if I'm having another heart attack or just an idea. I wish I knew.'

'So do I. Your ideas are bad enough.'

'What does that mean?'

'It means,' I said, 'that you don't *have* to climb rocks, just because they're there doesn't necessarily mean that we are. We're only half there – the other half is on *hold*. It also means that if you're thinking about going to the Snake Temple tomorrow forget it. I'll take Ava myself. You stay here and rest.'

'Who do you think you are?'

'I see myself as the mayor of hearts, the governor of idiocy, the president of bad trips.'

'I'll do whatever I feel like doing!'

'And do you think that Ava and I will *feel* like transporting your body half way across the world, accompanying the corpse, assisting at the formalities of heaving it onto one plane and sliding it off another, the sorrow, the *expense*! It's much, much more expensive to travel in a box.'

'You're sick.'

'We're both sick, and as for Ava; she has an order in for cholera, polio and viral hepatitis. I'm expecting one of them any day now.'

'I'm still going to the Snake Temple. It's not as if I had anything more strenuous to do than standing around observing. Do you think I'm going to scare myself?'

'You'll never, in your life see the Snake Temple. It has the ring of *doom*.'

'I'm sure statistics prove that more people are discovered dead in hotel rooms than in temples.'

'If you dare hazard one inch farther than Miss Kon Tiki's orchid basket in the lobby, I will take Ava's finger, plant it blindly to a spot on the map of the world – also in the lobby – and fly there tomorrow. You know that I don't hold up well under strain, that in severe crisis I usually veer towards epilepsy. Do I even have to mention the name *Beirut*?'

This was a traumatic collective memory of the time he took it into his head to accept an assignment in that capital of Levantine hell, and the way that Mother Nature forced me into demonstrating the scurrility of the idea: invisible tendons pulled me into the kitchen, wrapped my fingers around the fridge door handle and jerked. The next thing we knew there was yoghurt in the sink, eggs dripping from the ceiling, salami slices in the ventilation duct and beer cans were exploding like grenades against the bedroom door. Remembering, Pierre slumped on his side and blocked me out by grabbing the remote control and switching on a documentary concerning the fragile sexuality of pandas.

The multiple altars were garish, smothered in flowers and fruit. Invariably, in one gilded corner, plopped an immobile, turd-like reptile, casually stoned and unbothered by the featherbrained comments of the tourists. Maybe it was because of the little urns and trays of incense pellets that diffused black gusts of anaesthetising perfume, or maybe they were just holy; in any case they kept up a cataleptic guard over the chubby little Buddhas that twinkled in the candlelight. What exactly their role was I didn't know. Were they intermediaries, ombudsmen, tolerated devils, fallen angels? I would have liked to find out, for instance, what specific requests they were patrons of, and also the nature of those dark cakes scattered next to them.

Hash brownies, maybe? I never found out because every time I bent over to read the small paragraphs of explanation that were attached to the walls, voices, chilling and adenoidal, burped out, 'Fix yer pose, Sandy,' and 'I *like* this temple!' and 'Get a snapshot of the natives praying, Hart!'

It has to be television, that national blight, that gets this baby-voiced people high on drivel, and keeps them prattling for a lifetime, until their little flags are lowered at half mast to the strains of a tasteful dog food jingle. I'm not criticising. I'm *condemning* that side of America, 'The Most Beautiful Bimbo in The World'.

The big question remains: are great chunks of America *really* lobotomised? If they are, thanks a lot, NBC, CBS *et al*. So many tourists act as if they were speaking from a territory located somewhere between the skull and the face; thought goes no deeper. And what are those blissful bleeps and 'Howdy Doody' smiles? And why do they all have Mickey Mouse dangling from their ears, stamped on the jackets of their track-suits and engraved on their purses? I have never been able to understand that mouse and duck phenomenon.

Maybe Americans – on some intense cathodic plane – confound Mickey Mouse and that 'God' they're always going on about: he's good, he's asexual. He's adulated throughout the world. He's the source of infinite wealth. Is it possible that those stunted psyches, hatched in the radioactive warmth of the Tube, can actually go no further in their desperate spiritual quest than a benevolent *Mouse*? And if that sounds exaggerated, how much do you want to bet that there are more effigies with big black ears manufactured annually, than there are crucifixes, stars of David and crescent moons all put together?

Travelling around, I've often been startled by so many dinky American appreciations: 'Isn't the Acropolis like . . . hot!' Such low-brow motivations like, 'I only eat red, white and blue,' and that simple-minded, boy scout vernacular, 'My mom has a real neat backhand.'

The verbal regression is becoming so bad, I'm sure that before long there will be no more intelligent speech left, only scrambled Donald Duck gibberish.

Depressed by everything and everybody, I cut short our visit to the snakes. I wanted to go back to Pierre, but the taxi driver argued for the oldest Chinese temple in Penang, located on the road to the hotel. It was a place of riot –incense burnt at all levels, the air was thick with silver and black musky smoke. Literally hundreds of impatient believers implored statues for that two and a half cent raise, for an extra three inches of anything, or for other needs that I had never even dreamed of. In the chaotic front garden, crammed with shoes and offerings and dogs, an old woman, sooty and cold with inhospitable age, sat hunched under a wooden lean-to, massaging what should have been her feet if she'd had any. At the end of her legs were rounded stumps, about the size of muffins, trussed up in satin embroidered booties. Was I lucky enough to be seeing one of the last pairs of bound feet in the Orient? Maybe I could understand why Americans wanted to believe so much in a Divine Mouse. Maybe.

When we got back to the Kon Tiki, Ava ran straight from the taxi to the swimming pool to join her friends. I went to the desk to ring Pierre and tell him to come down for a drink, but the receptionist told me he was out and handed me a message. It said: 'Gone to the Snake Temple.'

One day later, the staff of a French fashion magazine arrived to shoot their annual bathing suit issue, using the hotel's kitchy exotica as background for modern living. We were just coming downstairs when the models breezed in. Precious, illusory, and unrecognisable as contemporary women: they were built like missiles, long, but at the same time compact, their raw material, a eugenic breakthrough. They wore intergalactic clothing made of extensible, synthetic fabric that stretched into the twenty second century and flashed all kinds of excellence across the lobby to the gawking *hoi polloi*, who suddenly became chastened in their conspicuous mediocrity. This was better than *Star Wars* – The Bionic Women Meet The Breakfast Buffet Beasts! While the lofty girls milled at the desk, indistinguishable from the potted ferns, the scattered groups of digesting, tenured guests stared crazily, their palates salivating in all directions.

In due course, Malaysian serving girls floated out to greet the mannequins. With the unruffled professionalism of decoy ducks positioned to lure in the greatly esteemed mallards, they melted together in recognition. I waited and watched until the last of them had disappeared into the elevator. In their wake erupted the worker bees; the stylists, the editors, photographers, make-up persons and gophers. A tidal wave of specialised enthusiasm lapped up against the marble walls and pillars of the hall; a deafening buzz of numbers, dates, measurements, requirements and orders drove us leftovers out towards the pool and the beach were we could gently efface ourselves.

It's half past five and I'm in the bar trying to convince myself that it's uncouth to order a Barracuda Tonic before six o'clock in the evening. I'm also listening to a pair of magnificent gazelles who are sitting next to me. They've been standing and posing since this morning, but they aren't tired: they're suspiciously giddy and excited.

'. . . that Bernard wants to share a room with me, but it's difficult to tell him, "Listen, in sixteen months my grandfather died and then my brother had the car accident and then my father and uncles died." I can see them in the room; I can feel them. I can't relax. I'm embarrassed'

These girls hurt the eyes; they're so perfect. It's disturbing to think that they just sprang up like that, with everything in place like a model home: their hair is hard and shining ceramic; their facial proportions from forehead to nose to upper lip remind me of nouvelle cuisine. Visible bones are everywhere but strangely rounded, refined, like very expensive wrought iron furniture – the flesh that covers them couldn't care less: it's nonchalant. I think I will have that Barracuda Sunrise, (or whatever they call those drinks) and try to assimilate all this. Is it true that men are dying? Is that what's happening to Pierre? Should I be nicer to him?

'What is *sam plus si*?'
'*Det.*'
'*Djet.*'
'*Djet.*'
'Good. And, what about *sam . . . plus sam*?'
'*Hok!* '

'Right. How old are you?'

'*Pet*, but I'm going on *kaow*.'

'Excellent! Are you sure you're not a Thai baby?'

'Hahahahaha!'

The day was so dark and cloudy that even with the large bay windows we didn't have enough light. To work we sat crouched under a suspended Tiffany lamp, its little KT stencils streaking non-mysterious writings on the wall. Because there were no interesting books about Malaysia or Penang in Ferringbi Beach, we concentrated on Thailand, the language and some history. The day before we had examined the nineteenth century royal court and its terrified subservience to the monarchs and their immediate families. One book told of a certain princess falling off a ceremonial barge and drowning because none of the servants were permitted to touch her or look upon her person. To tell the truth, most of the historical data was pretty gruesome. There were all kinds of provincial practices like smoking out uteruses after childbirth and piling up thousands of corpses during one of the many cholera epidemics and throwing them into the klongs. On the other hand they weren't any worse than a lot of fairy tales and they did capture the imagination.

'You remember what we read yesterday about the old Thailand'

'*Oui*, the mean maids.'

'They weren't mean. That's all they knew. Servants were taught to be like that.'

'Well, *I* would have disobeyed, and I would have saved the princess!'

'But, that's because you're modern, you don't have that problem . . . and also you watch TV and read books about Eloïse in the Ritz who goes around doing what she likes.'

'Were they sad when she died?'

'Probably not, King Chulalongkorn had seventy seven other children.'

'*Seventy seven*! Hahahahaha! Would you be sad if I had a heart attack?'

'You couldn't have a heart attack, Ava. Children never have heart attacks.'

'But would you be sad?'

'Of course! I would run back to Bangkok and throw myself into the crocodile pit. Any more questions?'

'Am I a homosexual?'

'What? How come you ask that?'

'We saw some ladies kissing at the beach and Daddy said they were homosexuals. That means *homo*, the same and *sexual*, sex. Am I?'

'I doubt it, but it might be too early to tell. Come back in a few years and we'll talk about it.'

'OK.'

The next day, we left the hotel, the island and the country. We now had to return to Bangkok for our flight back to Athens – presumably there would be seats during the week.

We were neither sad nor happy: having come for no particular reason, we were leaving, ditto.

Chapter Thirteen

Hully Gully Blues Keep On Shuckin'

On a pair of jeans that I had recently bought was a heavily stitched warning:

THIS GARMENT HAS BEEN SUBJECTED TO THE STONE WASHING PROCESS AND ANY IRREGULARITIES OF TEXTURE, COLOUR OR FASTENING ARE THE RESULTS HEREOF.

Our remaining week in Bangkok had such a 'stone-washed' quality about it; we felt beaten, thinned out, more wasted but lighter than other people – and we knew why. It was so hot that every step on the pavement meant wetness and otherworldly effort.

We checked into the YMCA, something of a landmark in the centre of town – an imposing middle class hotel with an Olympic swimming pool and Frank Sinatra's Inspirational Song Album piped into the lifts and halls. It was cool and spacious, giving off the puritan ethic that a guest would get as much comfort as a legitimate Westerner deserved and no more. The essentials seemed to be pile rugs, large beds, roomy bathroom, but no bar, no room service. It didn't matter: We needed the quiet and the refrigeration and that serious Protestant order to calm us down after snorkelling through those humid streets.

The first night we decided to investigate Patpong, the 'Lourdes' of the sexually handicapped, the convention grounds for The International Knights of Copulation: a road where the thick, oriental mist was the condensation of a thousand gallons of local and international sperm evaporating in the wake of its donors. 'Investigate' is a rather a strong word; it was more like 'stroll through' on our way to a Mexican restaurant situated in the heart of . . . the organ. I tried to explain it to Ava.

'You remember all those women we saw in Hua Hin that the men paid for?'

'*Oui*, you mean those playboy girls?'

'Right. Well, tonight we might see a lot of them in the street when we go to the restaurant.'

'*Et alors?*'

'Only it's much crazier at night, and maybe they won't be completely dressed.'

'*Et alors?*'

'Ava! Stop saying "So what?"! Anyway, it will be interesting. I just want to prepare you.'

'Will they be naked?'

'Probably.'

'Doing what?'

'Just walking around or dancing.'

'That's OK. Can I buy some Chicklet chewing gum?'

The tuk-tuk dropped us off on a side lead-in street, an expanding, contracting muscle of nervous trade, and before we even had time to lock arms, we were absorbed without discrimination, along with great hordes of sniffing men. We made up a rowdy battalion as we swept by girls who shimmied, be-bopped, twined, buckled, pirouetted, stretched, squatted and practically hung from lamp-posts in order to make an impression. Behind them, shyer sisters peeked out of tiny stores whose day-glo invitations were absolutely winning in their candour:

COME IN AND SEE HOW HARD WE TRY. . . ALL OUR LADIES ARE ROUND, FIRM AND FRESH FROM THE COUNTRY. . . TRY OUR TONGUE AND BUTTER MASSAGE.

Yokels slithered by ogling, whinnying and flapping their multiple appendages in response to the amazing creatures who smiled out from the curtains. I felt like a man myself, and I felt as if Ava were a small man.

The side road emptied into a main artery and this flowed underneath a pedestrian skyway criss-crossed with little ramps leading to darkened rooms. Extremely *Blade Runner*-glitzy below – sequined bras, metallic bikinis and other Wonder Woman apparel was on sale everywhere, suspended from racks and rustling like chimes in the night air – and furtive, squalid above. Glancing up, I could make out occasional flashes of lower anatomy, cigarettes and drained, male faces. Cassette outlets broadcasted the Patpong 'beat', most frequently an erotic meowing voice that pleaded, 'Ooohhhh . . . uunnnhh . . . unnnh, oooooh, take me, take me, take me, one more time tonight,' accompanied by a stereophonic, sighing electronic chorus.

Down the centre of this larger street, makeshift thatched bars offered bamboo stools and candlelight to clusters of western women, who sat hopefully, nursing gin and tonics, waiting for Harrison Ford to show up. Next to every bar was a scorpion and black widow spider vendor, hawking the world's ugliest souvenirs: they were big, seven inches long, and encased in glass frames laid out flat on the ground, to demonstrate a certain horizontal reality. I wondered how many times a drunken tourist had put his foot through the merchandise. The odd feeling in Patpong was of jollity. Other 'hot' neighbourhoods like Times Square or Pigalle were either sinister and/or dangerous, but here, everyone was a 'silly boy'.

'I lovvvvvvvve Silly Boys,' cooed a pumpkin breasted amazon, painted on a doorway. Cheerful pimps, reminiscent of *Guys and Dolls* ran out to salute Ava: one of them gave her a little cloth bracelet. The idling women yelled like auctioneers at Pierre, then winked at me as if I'd set it all up. Other G-string flaunters stood at corner grills, inspecting their shanks and grabbing the odd kebab. I was incredulous at some of the bodies: from ankle to waist one marble line curvy, yes, but no wrinkles at the buttocks or at the back of the knees. How did they do that? Maybe they only stayed vertical or horizontal, avoiding the less remunerative sitting position.

We stopped in front of a relatively accurate reconstruction of a Mexican hacienda. *Hola*! According to the outside menu, it was an oasis of hot tamales, chilli burgers, enchiladas, corn on the cob, bottled beer with howling wolves on the label and steaks that weighed as much as Pierre could lift. We pushed open the door and got punched in the ears with broad, complaisant, Northwestern whine. So much relief was going on here: hurrahs of vowel recognition and intoxicated pivots on the good old American 'R'.

With one quick look, I could tell that the room was divided into two camps: the businessmen, who looked like presidential candidates, and the college boys, who looked like presidential candidates. Into these parties we struggled, like cars out of gas, our *whoopee* capacity on empty. I thought we might be overcome by the gustiness of the place or torn apart by the explosion of 'Ho, Ho, Ho's. This trip had weakened us.

Then, as we wove among the fraternities of ajaxed elbows and madras shorts, a beer mug banged a nearby table and a voice yelled,

'Fair dinkum! Hello, love!'

The train station Australians!

'Hi!' I said. 'How was your trip? I never saw you in Hua Hin.'

I noticed that they'd latched onto a new mate, a Thai girl of any possible age, who would have been pretty, if it weren't for the green Betty Boop eyebrows that had been smudged with beer and now hung over her lids like crushed grasshoppers,

'Right!' trumpeted Davo. 'We never went. We took a boat to Koh Samui, instead. That's how I met Pornthrip, here.' He smiled at the girl and gave her a nudge with his elbow.

'Have a beer then! Is this yer old man – the one with heart? Bloody Oath! We thought you were an old bugger! Right, Reg?' Turning to Ava, he added, 'And this is yer ankle biter?'

I had the uncomfortable sensation that we were guests on a late-night Venusian talk show. We had been lengthily trained by NASA, but there were, nevertheless, gaps, spaces of mind violated. To make matters worse, I had never mentioned these particular 'brothers' to Pierre, standing beside me, stunned underneath his pallor, not understanding who these people were, much less, what they were saying. He tried hard to look affable, but this only gave him a Stan Laurel vacancy of expression that contrasted sharply with the Australian's grimaces of permanent deception,

'Pornthrip? Ankle biters?' I repeated like a student in a language lab.

'It's a common name in Thailand,' said Dave, 'even if it does sound sexy. She's a good sheila, the trouble is, she only speaks German. Ahhh! So what! She used to hang around with all these German blokes, see, so she didn't get time to learn English.'

Pornthrip squeezed his lizard tattoo good-naturedly and popped a corn chip into his mouth.

'Sit down! Sit down!' insisted the others as they requisitioned chairs from a next-door table of teenage realtors.

'Hey,' said Reg to Ava in an accusatory tone of voice, 'Yer a lucky little ankle biter, not going to school like the rest of 'em.'

She sat erect, seriously inspecting him to see if any of her self-esteem were at stake.

'I can read newspapers and speak Greek,' she announced for the record.

'Good on ya, kid!' shouted Dave, and then, 'What are ya, some kinda genius?'

'We live in Greece,' I explained.

'Yeah?' said Reg, 'Where's that then?'

Pierre decided to be a mate, 'On top of Africa, across from Italy and under Yugoslavia.'

'Right!'

They all look at him as if he, too, were a genius. We ordered some more beer, chilli and nachos and when they arrived, everyone more or less relaxed at the sight of equally distributed food and drink. We talked about our different trips, boats, trains. From time to time, Pornthrip let go a '*Kook mal*', causing Dave to thump her as if she'd told a very good joke. Only Rhonda was sullen, barely opening her mouth, except to inhale the head of her lager. Later, I found out why.

'Is Pornthrip travelling with you?' I asked after racking my brains for mutual vocabulary words.

'Yeah,' she hissed, 'a little too far, if you want to know what I think. He's bloody takin' her back home with him.'

'But they don't speak any common language! They can barely understand each other!'

'Yeah, she's a stupid moll.'

'Oh well,' I tried, 'she'll learn English soon enough when she gets to Australia.'

'When pigs fly, she will.'

When we'd finished the chilli, when Reg tried to force Pierre into smoking a Winfield (scoffing that a simple cigarette never killed anyone), when Dave started caressing Pornthrip's belt buckle, and when Rhonda – goaded into some outback, upfront rebellion – picked off the scab on her freckled upper arm and dropped it into her uneaten taco shell, we bid adieu to these strapping acquaintances, wishing them luck when they finally 'settled down'.

Although we would never cross paths again, their goodbyes rang out with promises of frequent contact.

'See you,' said Rhonda.

'Catch y'around then,' said Reg.

'*Auf Wiedersehn*,' offered Pornthrip.

But Dave put it best, with a simple but poignant, 'Cop-u-later!'

Two days into the city and the Bangkok woes pursue me over the steaming, spit-covered pavements that seem to bubble and heave in the molten afternoon. There is a gut-niggling sensation of 'No Future' working its way down my stomach. Self-appreciation is at an all-time low; what am I doing among five hundred million tuk-tuks? Where is the dignity in six inch underarm stains? I have a feeling, however, that if I can possibly get to the glorious Wat Po temple, I will be made whole again. But it's 400 degrees in the shade and my ear drums are already reverberating from this morning's trip to the Bangladesh Airlines ticket office.

I am standing outside the YMCA, trying to be courageous, alone in Hades without Pierre and Ava who are upstairs, reading Le Monde *and* Archie *comics in their cool beds. I can't do this. But I do.*

The first thing that happens as I enter the gates of Wat Po is that I embarrass a busload of Korean tourists standing around me by crying – really sobbing my heart out: this is the most beautiful place I've ever dreamed of beholding! Superlatives such as 'gorgeous' and 'magnificent' are just so many grunts, unfit for the task. Up until now, the people who concoct adjectives have only toured such lesser wonders like glaciers, savannahs and Radio City Music Hall, without ever making it to Wat Po. I have to take on the shaky responsibility of unprecedented communication. The best words I can come up with, off-hand, are: stellarous, cosmifital, glinteloquent, awe-binding!

Do you know what meets the eye? Gilded domes and delicate towers encrusted with 50 acres of mirror chips and ceramic petals and mosaics of amethysts, mother-of-pearl and lapis lazuli. And more and more, forever, gold: a monopoly of deep, wise yellow, tithed from the earth. I can't help seeing gold, and when I think I've seen it all, really understood it, whoops, here comes gold again! Gold doors etched from massive ores and dragged here by behemoths. Filigreed windows of gold crossing gold, completed in a thousand nights. It goes on and on, unextinguished; the gold never stops, nor the curves of the domes, the columns and the belly of Buddha himself.

I slowly follow the signposts of Buddhist intention, this circuit of divine humour, which Zeus, Jehovah, Jesus and Allah – all notoriously lack. I barely have any strength left to assimilate the coloured, scalloped roofs, the sharpened ice-picks that scrape the sky, or to fully appreciate the flocks of demons and sprites, carved out of stone and wood, mocking and gleeful in every turn of the path.

I sit down and look through the tears that still wet my eyes. I try to pretend that this is my natural habitat, that the earth is a gently developed settlement of fawns, exquisite oxygen, and snakes that crawl around my waist to make belts. I dream that the words 'Republican National Convention' and 'Calvin Klein Underwear' are but phonetic exercises for sharpening the wits.

Then, finito, into my musings and line of worship sail the Family Swine, as unbelievable as this wat, as arresting as the Emerald Buddha. All thoughts of quintessence disappear like egg white evaporating in the wind. The wretched truly rule. I now contemplate the flip side of paradise: one man, or something; hefty, throaty, necky, middle-aged, wearing thick bifocals that contrast luridly with his blue six-o'clock shadow. He has an ugly expression screwed around his mouth in the way of skin around a wound. All he's doing is reading a guidebook and pointing to a turret, but he gives the impression of Mengele showing the way to the experimental laboratory.

His wife on the other hand, is a fading cheerleader, all curled up at the edges, though she doesn't know this yet. She mistakenly emits short vibes of gorgeousness, which the hypotenuse from her chin to her throat wobblingly belies. Her dainty, eraser-like nose, checked in expansion by a hard little septum, is too small for the rest of her development – but she realises its importance, it keeps her coy. The nose is a dictator that determines the accessories: hair as in Sunkist lemons (billowing pony-tail of the stars), lips like jelly beans, and the halter neck rejuvenating mischievous breasts that peep out and signal, 'We were cheerleaders, too!'

This couple has propagated intensely, horribly. They are answerable for two, giant, crew-cut teenagers who look like twin Henry Kissingers, and one sweet piece of jail-bait – a little girl about Ava's age – her teased hair indented horizontally by a plexiglass walkman that she's smartly attached to her Peter Pan training bra.

Well, this type of apparel is common enough in the ever-flowing parade of the Damned, but the dunces before me are singular: the males are bare chested, meaning ash-white Crisco beneath Yeti-like pelosity (worn as medals) and all are wearing microscopic short-shorts that slice their buttocks halfway up the cheeks, exposing pounds and pounds of arse cleavage. They are also sporting baseball caps that say, 'University of Wisconsin'.

Do tourists think? Is there some typographical error in one of the big guidebooks that makes people believe that Thailand is a nudist camp? This is supposed to be a sacred place, there's a sign at the entrance which asks visitors to dress decently – but this tribe is clearly exercising its fundamental right to wander the earth gathering nuts and fruit. I might as well abandon the idea of any Buddhist tranquillity – my despair is too hectic.

Outside each temple gateway are piles of shoes: the flip-flops of the Thais and the bigger, flashier furniture of the leather-shod voyager. It's always surprising to see them there, in such great variety: imported, modest, cockeyed, threadbare, dainty, their shapes sentimental somehow. I take off my own sandals, reluctantly; according to the Bangkok Post, *there have been recent incidents of shoe theft all over town and it's disturbing to imagine being without protection on these burning streets, hopping over spit and tiptoeing through tuberculosis. But I do take them off. I'm not from Wisconsin.*

That night we went to the Siam Intercontinental to get a drink before hitting the klongs for dinner. This hotel was a tropical city; it had its own private jungle of lush foliage, landscaped ponds full of obese goldfish, live, haughty cranes, peacocks: I wouldn't have been at all surprised to encounter a stray leopard.

We ambled in the sunset to the pentagonal swimming pool, already lit up for the night and reflecting the bungalow apartment units where we could see the shadows of airline executives and orthodontists relaxing. We pushed onward through the flowers and well-spoken parrots until we got to the front veranda with a brass plate saying, 'Bar and Coffee Shop With Various Noodles At Your Disposition'. What a nice way of putting it, I thought. At the end of the terrace was a post-modern Cocktail and Concert Lounge, a trifle smaller than the Guggenheim Museum, its tsarist staircase a runway for princess wives in noisy aluminium haute-couture. We walked a few furlongs over semi-precious tiles and finally sat down on a couch made out of newborn baby calf hide.

After examining the list of drinks, we ordered a 'Suffering Bastard', a 'Velvet Unicorn' and a 'Shirley Temple' from the waitress (a *suma cum laude* of some very prestigious charm school) who lovingly presented us with crystal bowls of popcorn, plates of salmon roe canapés, and green olives laid out on crushed ice. The Jimmy Bell combo struck up 'I Just Called To Say I Love you', impelling a couple of tipsy matrons behind us into a finger-snapping back-up. Halfway through the number a successful New York voice boomed from the shadows,

'Hey Craig, you see Stevie Wonder's new wife? Neither has he! Ha! Ha! Ha! Get it?'

The hurrying surface of the klong regaled us with mementoes from *all* Bangkok; wood, straw, soggy ice cream cones, clothes, rice paper, hair, faeces. A witch's brew of material whizzed by, casting a rank odour into a night air already heavy with coal smoke, incense, honeysuckle, Mekong Whisky and sweat. In the car park turned piazza in the evening, amongst multitudes of Thai families, working men and shop-girls, it was half past ten and an easy 100 degrees. My blouse, which had been pink when we started out, was now deep red with perspiration and Pierre's hair was plastered back in a sleek Al Capone 'do. We weren't too disturbed by this – after our drinks and a bottle of whisky and a few beers thrown in for good measure.

'We should have drunk more on this trip,' complained Pierre. 'It's the one thing the doctor said I could do, and we didn't even take advantage of it.'

'He didn't say I could drink! I certainly don't regret non-existent hangovers in this weather. Imagine the atmospheric tonnage inside your head at nine o'clock in the morning! I'm *soooo* glad I didn't drink.'

'It would have been something to do; nursing a hangover keeps a person busy.'

'Come on, it hasn't been that bad!'

'Speak for yourself! You've been simulating adventure like an Amstrad video game everyday, it's been one thing after another.'

'That's life, Pierre.'

'That's desperation! This was supposed to be the trip we'd been planning for ten years – a visit to the Thai, Malaysian and Indonesian *people*! A cultural dream . . . You can't imagine what we've missed!'

'So we had bad luck! But even at the worst of times there was still something going on. What did you want us to do, spend two months in an oxygen tent? At least we saw a few things. We found out that Swedish women's fingernails fall off in Stockholm, that the Chinese pop their napkin bags after a good meal, and that the Thais make pilgrimages to the statue of Queen Victoria in the North to pray for fertility.'

'You read that in the *Bangkok Post*.'

'*Et alors?*'

As usual, on the few sporadic occasions that we drank, Ava felt a liberating undercurrent and was off under the trees, whirling and twirling with a group of children. I was too dazed to realise that, from time to time, she was rolling around on the ground, breading herself in disease. My maternal caution was definitely a white collar nine-to-fiver that didn't take overtime with good grace. It had been a pleasant evening, from the frosted glamour of the Intercontinental to the steamy 'people's' barbecue – it was an inverse sauna, leaving us red and glowing, with a little help from our blends.

Under the black and purple shadows of a gnarled tree. Ava and her *amigos* did acrobatics. First, the lotus position, then, walking on the knees with the feet pushed up against the thighs, near back bends, legs twisted like strudel dough. A young man came around selling pictures of the king. There was nothing wrong with this trip.

It was Pierre's ardent inclination to float down the central klong just before sunset, and take in the light of the city's energy – 'a diamond', he rhapsodised, 'reflecting in a cesspool.'

I agreed with the 'cesspool' part: a klong is to a river what halitosis is to a baby's breath – a question of bad habits. From time immemorial, the klongs had been used as automatic garbage disposal units, handy municipal sewers and floating cholera dispensers. There was a strong family resemblance to the Styx.

We had to pass through a creaking pierhouse that was jammed with the obligatory vats and cauldrons, plus other uncoordinated merchandise: butcher knives, paper flowers, basketballs, tin puppets, bicycle tyres. In Bangkok, wherever there was the slightest possibility of assembly – in queues, or at red lights, or even in front of restaurant toilets – scramble, scramble, scramble, business precipitated like ants around crumbs. I couldn't stand free – ever – or stare into oblivion, without somebody waving a Sony electric toothbrush in my face. If I tried to move away, I would find myself in the middle of an eight thousand decibel Nirvana cassette demonstration. I'm not complaining, just recalling. People can have mixed recall – can't they?

The only difference between this market and other bazaars was that here, the vendors were swaying softly, like the Mormon Tabernacle Choir, lulled by the rocking wooden planks and the rhythmic lapping of the river, a few centimetres from their feet. Occasionally, a Coke and Pepsi salesman would stand over a gap between the boards and jiggle a waste bin of crushed paper cups and mangled straws, until one by one, they all trickled into the brown gravy that carried them away – poor men's apple blossoms floating out to join the great flotilla of excreta.

We tried to buy tickets from a young woman who was breast-feeding a baby in her arms and restraining a toddler with her foot, all the while absorbed in a pornographic comic book. The cover was an illustration of a naked female skydiver who glided over a field of supine, nude soldiers, 'saluting' as it were. We had to remind this person that she was supposed to be a ticket agent, and that we weren't there to ogle at her magazine. Her head came up groggily as if she'd just opened her eyes after ten minutes of shampooing, and she demanded 250 baht – exorbitant for transportation of any sort. We thought we were being ripped off, but Pierre checked the official printed rates and saw that, for the boat he wanted – an individual outboard 'gondola' – it was *the* price, so we paid and went out to wait on the dock.

The river was very high. There didn't seem to be the correct, diplomatic distance between the water level and us, as if we were being threatened or bullied – although by now I knew that this was a major part of Third World come-on – manifestations of nature that were always extreme: if it was a leaf, it was a green leather bathmat; a common flower was like a New Year's Eve party hat; even the rare French fry had the tumescent look of a peeled banana.

This river was a rushing, *high*, gulping, oriental, liquid drink, swaying at its edge. No problem.

Houseboats, or rather hutboats, tried to squeeze each other out of front position along the banks, but many of them got pushed sideways or shooed into the corners of the wharf. Jerry-built constructions, conceived on the façades of abandoned warehouses, grew forward on stilts, until they nosed their way in among the boats. From the decks dedicated mothers cooked away the afternoon, glancing indifferently at their children, who were actually diving from the prows and the piers into the septic klong. As we watched in dismay, little boys jumped like electrocuted frogs into the fermenting custard of slime, litter, scum, spittle, urine and oil slick. Their game was to do a bull's-eye into the nucleus of the closest shit-float and to emerge through the same passage, their heads bobbing amid rusty cans and other unmentionables. When they swam back to their diving posts, we could hear *trick . . . plunk . . . splatter . . . thunk*, as the hands and arms crashed through the debris. Then, to add immediate danger to long-term danger, a lance-shaped, outboard motor-powered canoe bore down on the splashing children, forcing them to lunge desperately, left and right, to keep from being skewered alive. This James Bondian devil turned out to be our water taxi. The driver, after jumping out to consult the prurient ticket-mother approached and invited us to join him.

From the moment I put my foot on board, I had the feeling that this was just not 'done' – that the physical etiquette was all wrong. To begin with, the boat was a temperamental lightweight about five metres long, with the bulk of the charge – three passengers plus gondolier plus sputtering diesel motor – on the tail end. This meant, of course, that the long front before us was sticking up like the middle finger of an angry fist and that we 'sea-dogs' were huddled below like three knuckles and a thumb.

When we took off, the thrust of the engine's first efforts submerged us at least 15 more centimetres, so that the hideous, lurking miasma of the klong was only a hairsbreadth from the edge of the boat. If you still don't get the picture, then try to imagine a submarine propelled into battle: well, my head was the periscope – since I was sitting in the foremast – and behind me, Pierre and Ava were Gregory Peck and Mickey Rooney, the courageous officers in charge. As we picked up speed, the front began to bounce and slender blades of river casually loped over the sides, spraying us with a musky, pestiferous toilet water.

The heart attack, the daily tension, the polio scare, the Penang rat, were so many episodes of *The Bill Cosby Show*, compared to this experience of joy-riding through diseased swill, and the slow, awful understanding that we were now going to race with another taxi, not six metres away. Its own passengers were a knot of dishevelled Thais, waving at us and cavorting like teenagers. I looked back at Ava who was grinning crazily, and at Pierre whose eyes were half shut in delight. I wanted to scream out for the driver to stop, but I held myself in check – for once, they were having a good time! I had to exercise some restraint; after all, nobody else in our boat or the other boats appeared to be afraid. I tried to pray. *Oh Buddha, please don't let this boat jump out of the water again and land with a thud. Please make sure that the only germs that reach us are one or two of the following: flu, common cold, fever blisters or eczema. But if we have to catch a major illness, could it simply be malaria?*

Oh Buddha, can't you possibly shelve the typhoid, meningitis, polio and cholera? If we survive this excursion, I will – say, within the next six months – promise to take into careful consideration, the idea of converting to Buddhism. I will also put 200 baht into the collection basket the next time I pass a temple. Please give the captain of this ship a revelation of serenity, or at least make a little something go wrong with the motor that will render bouncing inadvisable.

At the end of the prayer we lost sight of our competitor, who shot ahead in a championship manoeuvre, but a few minutes later we came alongside a large passenger ferry, teeming with pink foreigners in flattened sailor hats and coloured visors. We indulged in a lot of reciprocal squirting and when we were halfway past them an army of cameras started clicking at us while an urbane bald-headed man yelled, 'Ahoy, Ahoy'.

I thought that we were now racing the big boat and that our driver was showing off his speed, that we would be far ahead in a matter of minutes, but this was all wrong because what he had in mind was to play 'chicken' with his big brother. Before I could even croak, we had skimmed his starboard side by a millimetre.

When I looked up towards the steering cabin of the ferry, I could see the captain sponging his face in appreciation. Mercifully, our impetus slackened and I thought *It's over!* Buddha was handling the situation.

In fact, our boat was stalling, biding time for the ferry to advance, so that we could start all over again.

Very, very unhappy, I turned around, and waving big X's with my arms, tried to yell for our captain to slow down. Pierre watched me as if I were a blue-haired grandmother that had just dropped out of the sky. He had to cup his mouth and bellow to be heard above the noise of the motors and the splashing.

'Whaaaaaaaaaaat's the maaaaaaaatter?'

'We'eeeeeere goiiiiiiing to caaaaaaaapsiiiiiiiiize!'

'Thaaaaaaaaat's impooooooooosible!'

'Maaaaaaaake hiiiiiiiiim stoooooooooop!'

'We'eeeeeeeeere ooooooonly haaaaaaaving fuuuuuuuuun!'

'Thaaaaaaaaaat's whaaaaaaaaat Riiiiiiiicky Neeeeelsooooon saaaaaaaid wheeeeeeeen hiiiiiiiis plaaaaaaaane craaaaaaashed!'

But Pierre didn't do anything because the ferry abruptly turned left to the dock and we slowed down to a normal port police speed, no other mates on the horizon. By then, all our underwear was visible, which is what happens when you soak diaphanous material.

We've been back in Greece for almost a year now and not one of us has ever had so much as a skin rash, although this might be due to our having zoomed directly to the mighty, occidental taps of the hotel shower, our taxi driver honking madly as I urged him on. I still haven't become a Buddhist: I don't think my personality would be very compatible with their precepts – I mean, I don't think I would *add* anything to that particular religion.

My last consummate Bangkok experience had a name: 'Robinson's'.

It was a flashy Japanese department store in the centre of town – a mercantile combat zone wherein raged battles of diverse greeds and frustrations. I only wanted to buy a pair of reading glasses, but I ended up casing the whole building. Dazzled by the goods, stunned by the prices, intrigued by the anomalies, and finally, sanguinary – bloodthirsty – ready to kill, maim, disfigure any woman wearing a 'Robinson's' badge who offered to help me, sir.

The instant I walked in I knew I was going to get shopping sickness, that mild nausea brought on by the constant eye movement it requires to scan an array of articles, their sizes, colours and relative worth. Here, it would be exacerbated by the mountainous quantities of products – and their feeble prices – wee, puzzling amounts having nothing to do with economy, import taxes or trade balances, little vestigial figures hanging there for no concrete reason. I began to waver at the first jewellery counter: gold, silver, pearls, platinum dangled for the taking. I could have grabbed a fistful and told the saleswoman to wrap it all up. At these prices, you didn't have to choose.

'Take it easy!' I warned my Visa card hand. 'You've just arrived. Walk around, don't get carried away with ground floor play.'

Expecting miracles, I loaded my excitement onto the escalator and as we rose I had a panoramic view of the first level: incalculable merchandise – whole squadrons of clerks, seven or eight to a cash register, long, swelling freeways of black-haired customers and punctuating this commercial rally, intermittent knots of big, hard-breathing foreigners, awkwardly advancing.

On the first landing four salesgirls doggedly wrapped themselves around my body and tried to force me into unnatural acts. They rubbed against my blouse, they purred, they moaned. They tried to rip off what I was wearing and force me into the garments they wanted to sell. They told me that my belt was 'cute', that I had 'big eyes', that my curls were 'so nice', that my shoes were 'blue'. *Why were they allowed to do this? And why were they slipping that transparent Marilyn Monroe shorty nightgown over my head?* I squirmed, feigned a left shoulder thrust, moved to the right and was able to flee.

Other employees guarding the sidelines eyed me ambitiously, trying to anticipate my moves but I kept walking fast, strategically altering my path until I reached a cool, less congested outpost. I felt a certain exhilaration at having thwarted them, but my victory was brief: I had wandered into the Valley of Creepy Dolls – the Cosmetics Department.

The Thai chapter of this vain sisterhood consisted of two dozen dragon ladies, varying in age and layers of foundation. They called out to me in modulated voices, 'Excuse me, you skin very dry skin. You like Nutritional Vitamin Humidifier?' and 'We have all make-ups for you lady. No make-up, no good. You no beautiful! Come here please!'

The only thing that made it bearable was the ravioli and noodle stand that had elbowed its way in between Helena Rubinstein and Estée Lauder; hot clouds of steam fogged the glossy lipstick posters and a fragrant melange of fish sauce, bergamot, musk and garlic wavered in the air. In this mist each salesperson had her noodle bowl, either nearby or directly under her nose, the porcelain soup spoons clicking against one-inch fingernails.

The second floor was a hushed chapel of select women's raiment: silk, linen, suede, shantung – all the material that causes reverence in experienced shoppers – wafting on the racks, provoking lust and desire. Almost immediately I spied *it*: a red linen sheath with a black and red bolero that looked as if Rita Hayworth were still in it. I gasped in recognition and ran over like a woman finally reunited with her sister after 20 years of separation behind the Iron Curtain. Instead of grabbing a hand I clutched the price tag. Instantly, a negotiating body squeezed in between me and the dress.

'You want? You like?'

I pointed to the dressing room. She bowed. We marched to the cubicle. She went in, turned on the light, hung up the dress and sat down on a stool. I stopped outside the curtain, not quite sure of what was happening. *Was she having a heart attack? Wasn't she coming out? Was I supposed to go into that cramped space, nose to belly with this individual? I baulked; nowhere in the world – except perhaps for Buckingham Palace – did this happen.* I made a diplomatic 'after you' gesture. She laughed. I folded my arms; she clapped her hands. I turned and walked away. She ran after me singing, 'Wisa card! Wisa card!'

I decided to wander around, wear her down, but I was helpless against the reinforcements; wherever I walked a new obstacle would block my way, would come and park itself in front of anything chooseable. Or they would shove something queer into my hands, something you could play shuffleboard in on a world cruise for Grey Panthers or something outrageous like a Davey Crocket feather and leather mini-dress. They would not lie down or be dissuaded, but kept up a running conversation in tiny chirping voices. It was out of the question to browse or even *buy*; I could only duck and run from these bobbing heads that kept appearing and reappearing and staring into my face like puppies panting after chopped meat. *My God, was this any way to do business – by sucking the client's bone marrow?* The Japanese, with their keen sense of negotiation, would be horrified to find out what was going on in one of their stores.

Or – was this a typically 'oriental' way of selling? Maybe with two hundred million shoppers pushing from behind, 'deciding' was simply not done. Besides that, these girls were poor and probably intent on escaping the armies of goons that were slobbering outside Robinson's windows, their noses squashed against the panes in anticipation.

I devised a plan: I picked out an ordinary white T-shirt costing peanuts and handed it over with my credit card. They were proud and happy to deal and so eager to record the transaction that they left me standing, unattended. I skipped to the original red dress, that beautiful heart breaker, slipped it off its padded blue hanger and went into the changing room. When I took the jacket off to try on the sheath I read – on the left breast – in big chartreuse letters – 'HAPPINESS IS A WARM PUPPY'. A weariness was setting in.

The third floor was the Daughters of the Universe Department, a quivering tribute to flower maidens and stubbornly traditional princesses. There were rows and rows of billowing white and pastel dresses and 'little miss' frocks with satin sashes and pastry sleeves. It was a majestic celebration of little girldom, and a really good hangout for browsers because you could hide behind acres of puffiness and the salesladies couldn't see over the racks. Unfortunately there was nothing Ava would be caught dead in – a Shirley Temple, taffeta party-dress with embroidered bib and ribbons?

On the side counters were silver sandals with crystal buckles and slinky, blue satin shorts for little Jean Harlows. Farther on; tutus, metallic pedal-pushers, leopard-skin blouses and panties that glowed in the dark. All of these articles had messages stamped or sewn or melted onto them: 'JUJU BABIES' . . . 'GIMME A BREAK' . . . 'FOXY LADY' . . . 'SWEETY PIE BREAKDANCE QUEEN' .

. . 'THE CHOCOLATE CLUB' . . . 'I'M DREAMING OF RAINBOWS AND ROSES'.

Who wore these things anyway? In the streets all you saw were prosaic shirt-dresses, neatly starched and as modest as uniforms. It didn't take long before I was detected by two breathless peddlers who dashed up to me crying, 'Mister! Mister!'

One of them jiggled a sweat shirt that said, 'MOUSE CONNECTION' while the other tried to make me pet a silver bowling jacket graced with the image of Cindy Lauper. From her wide pink mouth a comic strip bubble screamed, 'HULLY GULLY BLUES KEEP ON SHUCKIN''.

This was disgusting; gibberish had become decorative, like duelling scars on German students: something nasty slashed across one's person. I had a mind to go back, buy that dress downstairs, then cut out the offending nonsense, leaving a gaping hole that I would parade in a personal war against blabbing, loquacious clothes.

I could feel myself getting ill now and exactly when I needed it, I happened upon the Sushi Corner. (Time out for a personal message to sushi and sashimi lovers everywhere: it *does* exist, a cheap place where you can eat your fill, a repository of white fish, raw tuna and squid – not to mention an assembly line of sake carafes – as much as you want, and you don't have to hand over a month's salary.)

When I emerged 30 minutes later I felt like I'd tackled a Thanksgiving turkey single-handed, I was also reeling from the alcohol, my exposed skin flushed and all my freckles singing 'Auld Lang Syne'.

The last floor contained what I had come for in the first place – glasses – and I wasn't disappointed: New Wave. Old Wave, traditional, professional, vestal, brazen: I had my choice. A senior sales valkyrie approached me.

'You want some pairs of glasses?'

'That's right.'

'Here,' she said and without turning her head she reached behind her and swooped up a pair sitting on a show stand. I ignored her and fingered some thin, black rectangles.

'These no good. These for very businessman.'

I tried them on.

'I *am* very businessman,' I said, staring her down through the mirror.

'You nice, beautiful. Wisa Car?'

'*Wait!*' I held her at arm's length, I honestly needed glasses and I wasn't going to be discouraged by these offensives. She'd have to run around the block or take a cold shower while I was deciding.

'Look,' I said loudly. '*Chair*. Sit. *Sit!*'

She examined it and shook her head.

'*Sit!*' I repeated.

She moved closer and whispered, 'Maybe good red, black no good you.'

One thing was sure, these women were mutants of quality: as passive and frail as they were, they could, in spite of it all, hang on, encrust, grow roots, sprout buds. By now I was very angry . . . and drunk.

'Don't look at me! Go away! *Sit down!*'

I knew I was forsaking important poise but it would have taken the Royal Thai Army to make me stop. I had been to the cinema. I knew what build-ups were, and crucial moments when the main character falls to pieces. I felt warm and sick and weak – then – to my utter amazement, I heard oinking snorts coming from the bottom of my face, followed by outright bawling. I'm not proud of what happened next, but I won't disavow it: I stepped on her feet I couldn't see anyway to make her go backward, away from me so I simply put my feet on top of her feet. She didn't understand what was happening when she fell into the chair and I felt, through my tears, that the pleasant, middle class life I had lived up until then was over; this was the start of the declining 'snake-pit' years.

For a few infinite seconds my head swam and I felt like that Clemens back in Penang, when he met up with the branch from outer space. Insights lined up before me to be recognised: I was acting out an allegory of America's involvement in Vietnam: I was unfit to handle any situation that took place *out* of bed . . . if I wanted to I could continue to be aggressive. I could break glasses and knock down the mirrors and throw chairs around the room.

When I snapped out of this fury, I had another, more liberating flash; the saleslady wore a small gold and black tiger brooch pinned to her collar and, as she tried to balance herself, it flipped from side to side. With keen, alcoholic inspiration, I remembered a poem by William Blake: 'The tigers of wrath are wiser than the horses of instruction.' 'Ha, Ha!' I laughed, 'the horses of instruction!'

Miraculously, she sat there while I wiped my nose and tried to pretend it was all a joke. I was also hoping that there was no emergency buzzer under her chair which would rouse some kind of internal militia. I returned to the counter, cleaned my eyes and tried on more glasses, looking at myself obliquely, then head on – was I a middle-aged thug, or a near-sighted bitch? Should I get down on my knees and wipe her feet with my perm? Would my face bear rhinestones? Once in a while I checked her out but she wisely kept from moving. There were two pairs that I liked, the original black ones and some green striped things that turned me into a preying mantis – menacing but electric. When I took them over to her she was apparently glad to be back in the ball game and without any bad feelings, she led me to a small room where a technician had me read an eye chart. After this, they both escorted me to a waiting alcove furnished with two armchairs, a coffee table and 11 copies of the *National Enquirer*.

Before I knew it I was engrossed in an article concerning encounters with angels and how to recognise one on the street, and I only looked up to thank the saleslady for the complimentary glass of Cool Aid and the plate of chocolate chip cookies. It was as if America, smelling of Ivory Soap and Dentine, had crept up behind me, put her hands over my eyes, and whispered, 'Guess who?'

Two days later our plodyssey came to an end. We woke up in the morning feeling queasy around the pancreas, slightly euphoric and a little bit depressed. Our plane was leaving at 12 o'clock, destination Athens via Dacca, Dubai and other terrorist infested one-hour stands.

As we fumbled through the hours, we were strangely listless. The prospect of an international flight – usually the cause of happy speculation, hovered dully in the background like one of our Greek gas-lamps that needed a refill. Of course, any plan that included an aeroplane was, for me, tinted in hues of Edgar Allan Poe and Bette Davis. But this was something else; we should have been genuinely excited to be leaving – at least the climate – instead, we were glum. Pierre put it best: 'How can we be leaving a place when we never really arrived?'

And Ava second best: 'Do I have to go back to school?'

After getting dressed and packing our bags, we took the technically perfect, stainless steel Watsubishi elevator to the coffee shop for our last meal. In a desperate fit of loyalty, the three of us, anticipating future lack of nostalgia, ordered a Thai breakfast – beef soup and tea – and tried to pretend that it didn't bloat our stomachs up like water balloons.

We tried to make an estimate of this trip. What would turn out to be the indelible memories? For me, without even thinking, I knew it would be incense and excrement. It was a mixed odour omnipresent in every garden restaurant, behind food stalls, next to the klongs; it was all over Hua Hin and also in Penang. I think it was actually fertiliser and insect-repelling joss sticks – I hope it was fertiliser.

Pierre said,

'Fear. I was never in the army, I've never been attacked, I've always driven carefully. The only fright I ever experienced was once when I didn't have enough money to pay the bill in a restaurant. But here in Bangkok, and Penang, I felt I had a foot in the Orient and one in the grave; I thought there would be black and *adieu*. I won't forget the emptiness and greenness of the Saint Louis Hospital, the mosquitoes at night. And the geckoes on the wall chart.'

We looked at Ava.

'What I liked best were the Chicklets. You can't buy them in France or Greece, but here, even in the hotel you can get them. I liked the stray dogs in the temples because they live free and they can do what they want, and I liked the dogs on the beach that went swimming by themselves and those big spiders and scorpions, but I wish they weren't dead. It's not their fault if they have poison. It's their nature. It's not fair to kill them for souvenirs.'

It was time to go.

We step on the nothing that opens airport terminal doors. I am loaded with what will turn out to be 37 kilos of luggage; I'm dragging it on wheels and carrying it on my back and shoulders and arms. Ava is similarly burdened. Pierre has a Time Magazine *in his left hand. We walk to the check-in, looking at our feet, not really wanting to be here; we would prefer to be lying beside a swimming pool or jiving with monkeys or sipping 'Suffering Bastards'.*

The Bangladesh counter is swarming with awfulness: returning Europeans, decked out like amazonian rainbow birds, pushing clumsy pyramids of merchandise, shrilly victorious, hailing, comparing, and, in general, behaving idiotically. One French boy wears tight vasectomizing jeans and a hot-pink silk shirt, obviously custom-made. He poses. Two French girls, plain but noisy, sport large candy-striped shirts, rubber pop-art earrings, patent leather shorts, Mickey Mouse totebags and asymmetrical triangular wristwatches – all the things they'd dreamed of owning since they were 13 but could never before afford. An unlucky middle-aged secretary bashfully wears a Suzy Wong dress which probably looked dynamite on one of the Thai mannequins, but on her angular body the tight fitting back falls down in surprise over an absence of curves, while the rigorous, five-inch shoulder pads hoist her up and point her toward the overhead 'Duty Free' sign.

All of these people are engaged in irritating activities like: examining their passports to see how many countries are stamped, smoking thin brown cigarettes as if they were a bunch of Eric Von Stroheims, smearing on chapped lip balm and asking the hostess if the plane really is going to land in Dacca – because there are riots going on in Bangladesh and for the last couple of days, in pre-election rebel-rousing, they have been burning the capital and bombing official buildings. Wasn't the airport an official building? I wish these alarmists would just not ask: I'm scared enough to fly as it is and, in any case, the company will tell us lies.

I am now in a lunatic state of mind: miserable to leave, happy to encounter the Greek spring, unwilling to land in Dacca, and indignant at having to spend the next 12 hours with so many callous show-offs.

Pierre is leaning against the bay window of the departure lounge, yearning for the distant lead clouds that engulf the City of Bangkok, that mongrel place he hardly got a chance to see. Ava is drawing a picture of two aeroplanes in love. I swallow two Temestas and take a few long swigs of whisky from Pierre's pocket flask.

By the time we're in the plane and comfortably seated, my eyes scan all these new characters, my ears dilate in the direction of the nearest conversation, and, as a friend of mine from Chicago says after his seventh Bloody Mary: 'I'm nice.'

Epilogue

When we arrived in Athens, Pierre, on the advice of a Greek friend, went to see the 'biggest cardiologist in the world' who also happened to be Greek. This Titan, after a 15 minute interview, told him that he would advise immediate angiography and possible angioplasty, the only problem being that in Greece, you had to wait at least four months and then pay about $12,000 for each operation. Since Pierre still had medical coverage in France, he should go there *post haste* and get it over with.

In Paris he checked himself into the Pitié-Salpétrière Hospital: they gave him echographies and stress tests and bicycle tests, but the very competent doctors could find nothing out of order – neither scars nor murmurs nor blocked arteries.

'Frankly,' admitted one of the specialists, 'we think you simply had a *pericardité*, a kind of momentary infection that touches the heart. Anyone can catch it at anytime, but once you're over it, your heart is as good as ever.'

We returned to the island. The hills were covered in tiny spring orchids. All the cafés and taverns were overflowing, everybody was happy to see us – the aggravations of winter shrugged away. Pierre started smoking his five cigarettes a day. He now eats fried steaks with eggs on top. He pulls his boat out of the water like someone trailing a fur stole – and I haven't had to tell him a joke in the last seven months.